200 bread recipes

200 bread recipes

hamlyn **all color**

Joanna Farrow

An Hachette UK Company
www.hachette.co.uk

First published in Great Britain in 2009 by Hamlyn,
a division of Octopus Publishing Group Ltd,
2–4 Heron Quays, London E14 4JP
www.octopusbooksusa.com

Distributed in the U.S. and Canada by Octopus Books USA:
c/o Hachette Book Group
237 Park Avenue
New York NY 10017

Some of the recipes in this book have previously
appeared in other books published by Hamlyn.

ISBN: 978-0-600-62014-3

A CIP catalog record for this book is available from the
Library of Congress

Printed and bound in China

1 2 3 4 5 6 7 8 9 10

Standard level spoon measures are used in all recipes.

Ovens should be preheated to the specified temperature.
If using a fan-assisted oven, follow the manufacturer's
instructions for adjusting the time and temperature.

Eggs should be medium unless otherwise stated; choose
free-range if possible and preferably organic. The Food and
Drug Administration advises that eggs should not be
consumed raw. This book contains some dishes made with
raw or lightly cooked eggs. It is prudent for more vulnerable
people, such as pregnant and nursing mothers, invalids, the
elderly, babies, and young children, to avoid uncooked or
lightly cooked dishes made with eggs.

This book includes dishes made with nuts and nut
derivatives. It is advisable for those with known allergic
reactions to nuts and nut derivatives and those who may be
potentially vulnerable to these allergies, such as pregnant and
nursing mothers, invalids, the elderly, babies, and children, to
avoid dishes made with nuts and nut oils. It is also prudent to
check the labels of pre-prepared ingredients for the possible
inclusion of nut derivatives.

The publisher is very grateful to Kenwood, Morphy
Richards and Panasonic for providing the bread machines
with which the recipes in this book were tested: Kenwood
BM250 Rapid Bake Breadmaker; Morphy Richards Accents
Breadmaker; Panasonic SD 255WXC Breadmaker.

contents

introduction

Introduction

Bread-making machines are now one of the most popular and best loved "kitchen gadgets," producing freshly baked bread at the flick of a switch and with minimal effort on behalf of the baker. For purists, the process of mixing, kneading, and baking by hand is something that cannot be mimicked by a machine, but for most busy cooks a bread-making machine is a dream come true. What could be better than being able to program freshly baked bread, ready and waiting for you either at breakfast time or later in the day for snacks or sandwiches or to accompany a main meal?

This book contains a comprehensive assortment of recipes, from basic loaves to enriched sweet and savory breads, as well as gluten-free breads and recipes for teabreads and cakes. There are also plenty

of ideas for machine-made doughs, which are then layered, filled, shaped and baked conventionally, further extending the delicious range of fabulous breads that can be made with the machine.

ingredients

Most of the ingredients used in bread-machine baking are the same as those needed for making bread by hand, although for some, such as yeast, you will need to choose one specifically intended for bread-making machines.

yeast

Choose yeast that is labeled "instant" or "rapid rise." This yeast, available in ¼ oz envelopes or small jars, is designed for mixing directly with the other bread ingredients. (Fresh and dry yeasts have to be fermented with liquids before they are added to the other ingredients.) It is important that you use precisely the amount of yeast specified in the recipes: too little will prevent the dough from rising and too much will make it collapse during baking. Store yeast in a cool, dry place where it will keep for several months.

flours

For a well-risen bread with a light, airy texture use "bread flour," which is made from hard wheat and has a high gluten content. Brown or whole-wheat flour contains bran and wheatgerm, making a well-flavored bread with a nuttier, more fibrous texture. Because bran inhibits the action of the gluten, brown breads rise more slowly, and so the whole-wheat program on bread machines will be longer. Other wheat flours include malt and multigrain, which has added wheat grains, and this produces a well-flavored loaf with a slightly nutty flavor and a rustic texture. Spelt flour is an ancient form of wheat flour. Lower in gluten, it produces a closer textured bread but with a good flavor, and it can be used in most of the recipes that use white flour. Nonwheat flours, including barley and rye, have low gluten contents and, used on their own, produce a heavier textured bread. For lighter results, mix these flours with white bread flour.

gluten-free flours

Gluten-free flours are ideal for anyone who has an intolerance to gluten. Available from supermarkets and health food stores, they usually contain a mixture of different flours, such as potato, rice, and soy, in varying proportions. Some are specifically designed for use in bread-making machines and contain added natural gum, which helps imitate a more bread-like texture. Don't, however, expect gluten-free breads to taste like ordinary breads.

sugar

Sugar, which helps activate yeast, can be used in various forms, from superfine to brown, maple syrup, honey, or malt extract. If a large quantity of sugar is used, such as in teatime bread, the "sweet" program can be used so that the machine bakes at a lower temperature and stops the bread scorching around the edges. Do not use sugar substitutes.

salt

Salt is an essential ingredient in bread because it controls the rate at which the yeast ferments. If you don't like a salty flavor, use as little as half a teaspoon.

liquids

Unless you are using a fast/rapid bake program, liquids are always added cold to the bread pan. Water and milk are the most frequently used, but other liquids, such as fruit juices, cider, and yogurt, are sometimes

added for extra flavor. Don't use fresh milk if you are using the timer delay program on your machine as the milk is likely to sour. Use water instead and add a couple of tablespoons of milk powder with the flour, if desired.

enriching ingredients

Butter, oil, eggs, cream, and cheeses can be added to enrich doughs. Butter and oil also act as preservatives, keeping the bread fresher for longer. Use butter that's very soft rather than straight from the refrigerator, if necessary softening it in the microwave first. Do not use the timer delay program if you are using dairy produce or other perishable ingredients.

herbs, spices, and other flavoring

Chopped fresh or dried herbs, crushed or ground spices, and other flavorings, such as vanilla, saffron, and spicy pastes, can be used

to enhance the flavor of the most basic bread. Add the flavoring at the beginning of the program with the flour if dry or the liquids if wet.

machine programs

Selecting the right program is essential for good results. Bread-making machines vary in the choice of programs they offer, but those used in this book are the most often seen.

basic

This program is probably the most useful and the one you'll keep returning to. It's used for basic white breads or breads in which white flour is the main ingredient. Enriched sweet and savory breads can also be made using this program.

whole-wheat/wholemeal

Breads made using whole-wheat or wholemeal flours have a longer preheating time to allow the grains to soak up the liquid and expand, making a lighter, more aerated loaf.

fast/rapid bake

On some models this program can take as little as one hour, which is useful when you have run out of bread and need some fairly quickly. Unlike all other programs the water (or other liquid) is added warm to activate the yeast quickly and accelerate rising. Because the rising time is so short more yeast is used. The texture of these loaves is more dense and less aerated, but the bread

still has a good flavor. On most machines this program has only one crust option.

sweet

This program is used for cakes and breads that contain a high proportion of sugar. It cooks at a slightly lower temperature to stop the sugar burning.

cake

Use this program for yeast-free breads, teabreads, and cakes. Most machines include a mixing cycle, so all you need to do is put the ingredients into the pan and let the machine do the rest, which is ideal if your conventional oven is already in use. Because different models have different baking times, test to see if the cake is ready at the time suggested in the recipe rather than leaving it to the end of the program by which time the cake might be overcooked. Test by

piercing the center of the cake with a skewer: it should come out clean. Some bread-making machines don't incorporate a mixing cycle in the cake program, in which case you'll need to mix the cake ingredients conventionally, remove the kneading blade, and turn the blended mixture into the baking pan. Check with the manual first.

dough

This is a really useful program if you want to give your breads a personal touch by shaping, second rising, and baking them conventionally. It's also useful for breads to which you're adding a large amount of additional ingredients that would prevent a good rise if baked in the machine. The dough program is great for pizza bases, focaccia, sweet buns, and teacakes. You don't need to remove the dough from the machine as soon as the program finishes, but don't leave it too long or the dough might rise up over the top of the pan.

other features

raisin beep

On most models, the programs have a "raisin beep," which indicates when you should add additional ingredients, such as dried fruit, cheese, nuts, herbs, seeds, and so on, that you wouldn't want to get broken up during kneading. On some machines, whether you're baking bread or using the dough program, you'll need to select the "raisin beep" mode, as the machine won't automatically beep. Some models incorporate a raisin/nut

dispenser that can be filled beforehand, so the ingredients are automatically dispensed into the dough at the appropriate point in the program. If your machine doesn't have this facility, the additional ingredients can be added toward the end of the kneading cycle. Most manuals will provide a chart of how long the different cycles last, so if you're not in the kitchen you can set a timer to remind you when to add additional ingredients.

crust color

The choice of pale, medium, or dark crust is a matter of personal preference. Select the appropriate setting before pressing "start."

timer delay

This program gives you the choice of having freshly baked bread ready for you in the morning, after work, or a time that suits you.

13

Do not use perishable ingredients, such as milk, yogurt, and eggs. Consult the manual for selecting time delay options.

loaf size

Most bread-making machines offer three bread sizes:

• small—1 lb
• large—1 ½ lb
• extra-large—2 lb

Most of the recipes in this book are for 1 ½ lb loaves, and you should select this setting on the control panel before pressing "start" because the program times vary slightly, depending on the size chosen.

keep warm

Most programs have a keep-warm facility, circulating hot air for an additional 30—60 minutes after the bread is baked. For best results remove the loaf as soon as it's baked or at least within the keep-warm time. After this condensation will form inside the machine and the bread will soften.

adding ingredients

The ingredients should always be added to the bread machine in the order specified in the manual for your particular model, because adding them in the wrong order can result in failure. In most machines it's liquids first, then the flour, yeast, and sugar, but in some it's the other way round, with liquids added last. The order the ingredients are added is particularly important when the timer delay is used or the machine has a "rest" period before the kneading cycle starts, so that the yeast is kept separate from the liquids.

tips for success

• Measure the ingredients accurately. The wrong quantities of yeast, liquids, or solids will result in a poor loaf. Yeast measurements should be level, while liquids measured in a cup should be read at eye level.
• Take the pan out of the machine when you are adding the initial ingredients.
• When you are trying a new recipe check the consistency of the dough after a few minutes kneading. At this stage you can add (cautiously) a dash more liquid if the dough is dry and the flour is sticking around the edges of the pan or, if it's very wet, a little more flour.

- Extra flavorings that you want to remain in pieces, such as raisins and other dried fruits, roasted vegetables, olives, and fruit, are best added when the "raisin beep" sounds. If you add them at the beginning of the program they may get crushed and their texture and flavor could spoil.
- Use a plastic spatula to scrape down any dry dough that clings to the sides of the pan. Never use a knife or metal implement in the pan because you will damage the nonstick lining.
- Resist the temptation to open the lid once the program gets going. The draft of cold air will slow down the rising or baking and might result in a sunken loaf. Some of the recipes, however, do suggest brushing with milk just before baking and then closing the lid gently.
- Not all loaves have a domed crust after baking. Some enriched doughs, as well as low-gluten or gluten-free breads, often have a level crust or are slightly sunken.
- The kneading blade often comes out of the pan with the bread when you are shaking it out onto your work surface. Remove the blade as soon as it's cool enough to handle. If the blade remains stuck in position in the pan add a little water to the pan and allow it to soak for 5 minutes by which time the blade should be easy to remove. Don't put the bread pan in the dishwasher. Wash in warm, soapy water and avoid scouring pads, which will damage the nonstick lining.

- If there's a power cut or the machine is accidentally turned off during the program, turn the machine back on and the program should start again. If it's switched off for a long time, you might need to start again or finish baking the bread by hand.
- Remember that when you are removing cooked bread from the machine it's as if you were lifting it from the oven, and you'll need to wear oven mitts.
- Conventional bread recipes cannot be made in a bread-making machine because they contain a different proportion of yeast, flour, and liquids. Most conventional dough recipes can, however, be followed successfully, provided there's not so much dough that it rises up over the top of the pan.
- Breads made in a bread machine, particularly the more basic recipes, do not keep well and are best eaten on the day they are made.

basic breads

simple white loaf

Makes **1 large loaf**
Time **3–4 hours**, depending
on machine

1 cup plus 2 tablespoons
water
2 tablespoons **unsalted
butter**, softened
1 teaspoon **salt**
3 cups **white bread flour**,
plus extra for dusting
2 teaspoons **superfine sugar**
1¼ teaspoons **instant yeast**

Lift the bread pan out of the machine and fit the blade.
Put the ingredients in the pan, following the order
specified in the manual.

Fit the pan into the machine and close the lid. Set to
a 1½ lb loaf size on the basic white program. Select
your preferred crust setting.

At the end of the program lift the pan out of the
machine and shake the bread out onto a cooling rack.
Dust the top with a little extra flour and allow to cool.

For seeded cottage loaf, put 1¼ cups water,
2 tablespoons sunflower oil, 1½ teaspoons salt,
3 tablespoons each of sesame seeds, sunflower
seeds, and flax seeds, 3½ cups white bread flour, 1
teaspoon superfine sugar, and 1¼ teaspoons instant
yeast in the bread pan, following the order specified in
the manual. Fit the pan into the machine and close the
lid. Set to the dough program. At the end of the
program turn the dough out onto a floured surface
and cut off one quarter. Shape both pieces of dough
into rounds and place the larger one on a greased
baking sheet. Place the smaller round on top and
push a floured wooden spoon handle down through
both doughs. Cover loosely with oiled plastic wrap
and let rise in a warm place until almost doubled in
size. Bake in a preheated oven, 425°F, for 25 minutes
until golden. Transfer to a cooling rack to cool.

oat & buttermilk bread

Makes **1 large loaf**
Time **3–4 hours**, depending
on machine

½ cup **water**
¾ cup **buttermilk**
1½ teaspoons **salt**
2⅔ cups **white bread flour**
⅓ cup **steel-cut oats**, plus
extra for sprinkling
1½ teaspoons **superfine
sugar**
1¼ teaspoons **instant yeast**
milk, to brush

Lift the bread pan out of the machine and fit the blade.
Put the ingredients in the pan, following the order
specified in the manual.

Fit the pan into the machine and close the lid. Set to
a 1½ lb loaf size on the basic white program. Select
your preferred crust setting.

Just before baking begins brush the top of the dough
lightly with milk and sprinkle with extra oats. Close the
lid gently.

At the end of the program lift the pan out of the
machine and shake the bread out onto a cooling rack
to cool.

**For French toast with yogurt, strawberries, &
honey**, cut 4 thick slices of bread. Beat 2 eggs on a
plate with 3 tablespoons milk. Turn the bread slices in
the milk and allow to soak for 5 minutes. Sprinkle 2
tablespoons superfine sugar onto a plate and mix with
¼ teaspoon ground cinnamon. Heat 1 tablespoon
unsalted butter in a large skillet with 1 tablespoon
mild olive oil and gently fry the bread slices, turning
once, until golden on both sides. Turn lightly in the
spiced sugar and serve topped with thick yogurt,
strawberries, and honey.

multigrain bread

Makes **1 large loaf**

Time **3½–5 hours**, depending on machine

1¼ cups **water**

2 tablespoons **unsalted butter**, softened

1½ teaspoons **salt**

3 cups **multigrain flour**

1 tablespoon **brown sugar**

1¼ teaspoons **instant yeast**

Lift the bread pan out of the machine and fit the blade. Put the ingredients in the pan, following the order specified in the manual.

Fit the pan into the machine and close the lid. Set to a 1½ lb loaf size on the whole-wheat program. Select your preferred crust setting.

At the end of the program lift the pan out of the machine and shake the bread out onto a cooling rack to cool.

For fast-baked double wheat bread, put 1 cup plus 2 tablespoons warm milk, 2 tablespoons soft butter, 2 tablespoons salt, 1½ cups white bread flour, 1⅓ cups whole-grain spelt flour, 2½ teaspoons instant yeast, and 1 teaspoon sugar in the bread pan, following the order specified in the manual. Set to a 1½ lb loaf size on the fast/rapid bake program.

speedy sesame bread

Makes **1 large loaf**

Time **1–2 hours**, depending on machine

1 cup plus 2 tablespoons warm **water**
2 tablespoons **sunflower oil**
1 teaspoon **salt**
2 tablespoons **milk powder**
2 tablespoons **sesame seeds**
3 cups **white bread flour**
1 tablespoon **superfine sugar**
2½ teaspoons **instant yeast**

To finish
melted **butter**, to brush
sesame seeds, for sprinkling

Lift the bread pan out of the machine and fit the blade. Put the dough ingredients in the pan, following the order specified in the manual.

Fit the pan into the machine and close the lid. Set to a 1½ lb loaf size on the fast/rapid bake program.

At the end of the program lift the pan out of the machine and shake the bread out onto a cooling rack. Brush the top of the loaf with the butter and sprinkle with a few extra sesame seeds. Brown under the broiler, if desired.

For speedy three grain bread, omit the milk powder and sesame seeds from the above recipe and reduce the sugar to 1½ teaspoons. Replace 1 cup of the white flour with malted bread flour and another ⅓ cup with purple wheat flakes. Just before baking begins lightly brush the top of the dough with milk and sprinkle with extra wheat flakes. Close the lid gently and complete the program.

ciabatta

Makes **2 loaves**

Time **2–3 hours**, depending
on machine, plus standing,
shaping, rising, and baking

Starter

⅔ cup warm **water**

⅔ cup **white bread flour**

¼ teaspoon **superfine sugar**

½ teaspoon **instant yeast**

To finish

1 cup **water**

2 tablespoons **olive oil**

1½ teaspoons **salt**

2¼ cups **white bread flour**,
plus extra for dusting

1½ teaspoons **superfine
sugar**

1 teaspoon **instant yeast**

Lift the bread pan out of the machine and fit the blade.
Put the starter ingredients in the pan, following the
order specified in the manual.

Fit the pan into the machine and close the lid. Set to
the dough program. Turn off the machine before the
second kneading cycle and let the dough stand for at
least 4 hours.

Lift the bread pan out of the machine and add the
remaining ingredients. Return to the machine and set
to the dough program.

At the end of the program turn the dough out onto a
floured surface and cut it in half. (The dough will be
very sticky.) Using well-floured hands, gently pull the
dough into 2 loaves, each about 11 inches long. Place
them on a greased and floured baking sheet. Leave
in a warm place, uncovered, for about 30 minutes or
until about half as big again.

Bake in a preheated oven, 425°F, for about 20
minutes until golden and the loaves sound hollow
when tapped with the fingertips. Transfer to a
cooling rack to cool. Dust with flour.

For sundried tomato & herb ciabatta, drain and
thinly slice 1 cup sundried tomatoes in olive oil.
Roughly chop ¼ cup fresh mixed herbs (such as basil,
parsley, oregano, and thyme). Make the dough in the
machine as above using olive oil from the tomato jar
and adding the sliced tomatoes and herbs when the
machine beeps. Turn out onto a floured surface and
finish as above.

couronne

Makes **1 loaf**

Time **1½–2½ hours**, depending on machine, plus shaping, rising, and baking

¾ cup **water**
¾ cup **plain yogurt**
1½ teaspoons **salt**
3 cups plus 2 tablespoons **unbleached white bread flour**, plus extra for sprinkling
2 teaspoons **superfine sugar**
1¼ teaspoons **instant yeast**

Lift the bread pan out of the machine and fit the blade. Put the ingredients in the pan, following the order specified in the manual.

Fit the pan into the machine and close the lid. Set to the dough program.

At the end of the program turn the dough out onto a floured surface and shape into a round, then make a small hole in the center with your fingertips. Enlarge the hole with your fist until it is about 5 inches across and the dough ring is about 8 inches across.

Transfer the bread to a greased baking sheet and make 3–4 cuts across the surface (if desired). Grease the base of a small basin and put it in the center of the dough to keep the hole intact. Cover both dough and basin with lightly oiled plastic wrap and leave in a warm place for about 30 minutes or until it is half as big again.

Remove the plastic wrap and basin, sprinkle the dough with flour, and bake in a preheated oven, 425°F, for 20–25 minutes until it is well risen and browned and the bread sounds hollow when tapped with the fingertips. Cover with foil after 15 minutes if overbrowning. Transfer to a cooling rack to cool.

For easy sourdough bread, follow the recipe above using warm water instead of cold and Greek yogurt instead of plain. Increase the yeast to 2½ teaspoons. Set to a 1½ lb loaf size on the fast/rapid bake program. Just before baking begins, sprinkle the top of the dough with a little extra flour. Close the lid gently and complete the program.

walnut & honey bread

Makes **1 large loaf**
Time **3½–5 hours**, depending
  on machine

¾ cup **walnut pieces**
1½ cups **water**
3 tablespoons **honey**, plus
  extra to drizzle
3 tablespoons **unsalted
  butter**, softened
1½ teaspoons **salt**
2¼ cups **whole-wheat bread
  flour**
1 cup **white bread flour**
1¼ teaspoons **instant yeast**

Lightly toast the walnuts either in a skillet over a
gentle heat or under the broiler.

Lift the bread pan out of the machine and fit the blade.
Put the ingredients, except the walnuts, in the pan,
following the order specified in the manual.

Fit the pan into the machine and close the lid. Set to
a 1½ lb loaf size on the whole-wheat program. Select
your preferred crust setting. Add the walnuts when the
machine beeps.

At the end of the program lift the pan out of the
machine and shake the bread out onto a cooling
rack to cool. Serve drizzled with extra honey.

For mini pecan & maple loaves, lightly toast ¾ cup
roughly chopped pecan nuts. Make the bread as
above, using the pecans instead of the walnuts and
replacing the honey with 3 tablespoons maple syrup.
Use the dough program, cut the dough into 8 pieces,
and press into 8 greased ¾ cup individual loaf pans.
Cover loosely with oiled plastic wrap and let rise in a
warm place for 30 minutes. Brush with a little maple
syrup and bake in a preheated oven, 425°F, for about
20 minutes until well risen and golden. Serve drizzled
with extra maple syrup.

mixed seed bread

Makes **1 large loaf**
Time **3½–5 hours**, depending
   on machine

Dough
1¼ cups **water**
2 tablespoons **unsalted
   butter**, softened
1½ teaspoons **salt**
3 tablespoons **sesame seeds**
3 tablespoons **sunflower
   seeds**
3 tablespoons **flax seeds**
3 cups **malt flour**
1 tablespoon **brown sugar**
1¼ teaspoons **instant yeast**

To finish
milk, to brush
extra **seeds**, for sprinkling
   (optional)

Lift the bread pan out of the machine and fit the blade. Put the dough ingredients in the pan, following the order specified in the manual.

Fit the pan into the machine and close the lid. Set to a 1½ lb loaf size on the whole-wheat program. Select your preferred crust setting.

Just before baking begins brush the top of the dough with a little milk and sprinkle with some extra seeds (if desired). Close the lid gently.

At the end of the program lift the pan out of the machine, loosen the bread with a spatula if necessary, and shake it out onto a cooling rack to cool.

For seeded cheese batons, follow the recipe above but finely grate 1½ oz extra-sharp cheddar cheese and add to the machine with the flour. Set to the dough program. At the end of the program turn the dough out onto a floured surface and cut it into 3 equal pieces. Roll each piece to a sausage, about 11 inches long, transfer to a large, greased baking sheet, leaving enough space around the dough for them to rise. Cover loosely with oiled plastic wrap and leave in a warm place for about 30 minutes or until about half as big again. Use a floured knife to make diagonal cuts across the top of each baton and bake in a preheated oven, 400°F, for 15–20 minutes until risen and golden. Transfer to a cooling rack to cool.

boston brown bread

Makes **2 small loaves**

Time **1½–2½ hours**, depending
on machine, plus shaping,
rising, and baking

1 cup **milk**
5 tablespoons **molasses
syrup**
1 teaspoon **salt**
1 cup **whole-wheat bread
flour**
1 cup **white bread flour**, plus
extra for dusting
⅓ cup **rye flour**
⅓ cup **cornmeal**
1¼ teaspoons **instant yeast**

Lift the bread pan out of the machine and fit the blade.
Put the ingredients in the pan, following the order
specified in the manual.

Fit the pan into the machine and close the lid. Set
to the dough program. Thoroughly wash 2 empty
1 lb 10 oz tomato, new potato, or other large cans.
Place them on a baking sheet and grease and line the
cans as you would a cake pan.

At the end of the program turn the dough out onto a
floured surface and cut it in half. Shape each piece into
a ball and drop them into the cans. Cover loosely with
oiled plastic wrap and let rise in a warm place for about
40 minutes or until the dough reaches the top of the
cans.

Bake in a preheated oven, 400°F, for 25 minutes.
Remove from the cans and tap the bases. If the bread
sounds hollow it is cooked, if not return to the oven
for a little longer (but don't fit them back in the cans).
Transfer to a cooling rack. Dust the top lightly with a
little extra white bread flour and allow to cool.

For fruited Boston bread, roughly chop ½ cup
pitted dates or prunes. Make the bread using the
whole-wheat program, 1½ lb loaf size, and preferred
crust setting. Add the dates or prunes when the
machine beeps.

breakfast muesli bread

Makes **1 extra-large loaf**

Time **3–4 hours**, depending on machine

1¼ cups **apple juice**
1 large **egg**, beaten
2 tablespoons **unsalted butter**, softened
1½ teaspoons **salt**
2 tablespoons **milk powder**
1 teaspoon **ground mixed spice**
1⅔ cups **fruit muesli**, plus extra for sprinkling
2⅔ cups **white bread flour**
¼ cup **light brown sugar**
1¼ teaspoons **instant yeast**
⅓ cup **raisins**
milk, to brush

Lift the bread pan out of the machine and fit the blade. Put the ingredients, except the raisins, in the pan following the order specified in the manual.

Fit the pan into the machine and close the lid. Set to a 2 lb loaf size on the basic white program. Select your preferred crust setting. Add the raisins when the machine beeps.

Just before baking begins brush the top of the dough lightly with milk and sprinkle with a little muesli. Close the lid gently.

At the end of the program lift the pan out of the machine, loosen the bread with a spatula if necessary and shake it out onto a cooling rack to cool.

For fresh blueberry conserve, to accompany the bread, blend 1 teaspoon cornstarch with 1 tablespoon water in a small saucepan. Add 6 tablespoons apple or orange juice, 3 tablespoons superfine sugar and ½ teaspoon vanilla extract. Heat gently, stirring, until slightly thickened. Tip in 2 cups fresh or frozen blueberries and cook gently for 1–2 minutes until the blueberries soften and start to burst. Serve warm or cold, spooned over the bread and topped with thick yogurt.

fast-baked rye & caraway bread

Makes **1 large loaf**
Time **1–2 hours**, depending
  on machine

¾ cup warm **water**
¾ cup **Greek** or **whole milk
  yogurt**
1½ teaspoons **salt**
1 tablespoon **caraway seeds**
2 cups **white bread flour**
1 cup **rye flour**
1 tablespoon **superfine sugar**
2½ teaspoons **instant yeast**

Lift the bread pan out of the machine and fit the blade. Put the ingredients in the pan, following the order specified in the manual.

Fit the pan into the machine and close the lid. Set to a 1½ lb loaf size on the fast/rapid bake program.

At the end of the program lift the pan out of the machine and shake the bread out onto a cooling rack to cool. Serve thinly sliced.

For toasted rye & smoked trout sandwich, mix ¼ cup cream cheese with 3 oz skinned and boned smoked trout and 1 finely chopped scallion. Mix 1 tablespoon chili-infused oil with ¼ teaspoon superfine sugar and 1 teaspoon wine vinegar. Lightly toast 2 slices of rye bread and sandwich with the trout mixture, a handful of watercress leaves, and the dressing.

brioche

Makes **1 loaf**

Time **1½–2½ hours**, depending on machine, plus shaping, rising, and baking

3 **eggs**, beaten

⅓ cup **unsalted butter**, softened

¼ teaspoon **salt**

1½ cups **white bread flour**

2 tablespoons **superfine sugar**

1 teaspoon **instant yeast**

egg yolk, to glaze

Lift the bread pan out of the machine and fit the blade. Put the ingredients in the pan, following the order specified in the manual.

Fit the pan into the machine and close the lid. Set to the dough program. Thoroughly butter a 3 cup brioche mold or a 2 lb loaf pan.

At the end of the program turn the dough out onto a floured surface and cut off one quarter. Shape the larger piece into a ball and drop it into the brioche pan. Push a deep, wide hole into the dough with your fingers. Shape the remaining dough into a ball and press it gently into the indented top. (If you are using a loaf pan shape the dough into an oval and drop it into the pan.)

Cover loosely with oiled plastic wrap and let rise in a warm place for 50–60 minutes or until almost doubled in size. Mix the egg yolk with 1 tablespoon water and gently brush over the dough. Bake in a preheated oven, 425°F, for 20–25 minutes or until deep golden and firm. (Cover the loaf with foil if the crust starts to over-brown.)

After baking leave the bread in the pan for a few minutes, then shake out onto a cooling rack to cool.

For baby chocolate brioche buns, make the dough as above and divide it into 8 pieces. Push ½ square semisweet chocolate into the center of each piece and seal the dough around the chocolate. Space the buns well apart on a greased baking sheet. Cover loosely with oiled plastic wrap and let rise in a warm place until almost doubled in size. Glaze and bake as above, reducing the cooking time to about 15 minutes.

date & malted barley bread

Makes **1 large loaf**

Time **2¾–3½ hours**, depending
on machine

1 cup **milk**, plus 1 tablespoon
to brush

5 tablespoons **date syrup** or
malted barley extract

2 tablespoons **unsalted
butter**, softened

1 teaspoon **salt**

2 cups **barley flour**

1 cup **white bread flour**

1¼ teaspoons **instant yeast**

1 cup pitted **dates**, chopped

barley flakes, for sprinkling
(optional)

Lift the bread pan out of the machine and fit the blade.
Put the ingredients, except the dates, in the pan,
following the order specified in the manual.

Fit the pan into the machine and set to a 1½ lb loaf
size on the sweet program (or the whole-wheat
program if the machine doesn't have a sweet setting).
Add the dates when the machine beeps.

Just before baking begins brush the top of the dough
lightly with milk and sprinkle with barley flakes (if
desired). Close the lid gently.

At the end of the program lift the pan out of the
machine and shake the bread out onto a cooling rack
to cool. Serve buttered with breakfast preserves or
honey, if desired.

For spiced fruit loaves, add 2 teaspoons ground
mixed spice with the flours and set to the dough
program, adding 1 cup pitted prunes or dried figs,
chopped, (instead of the dates) when the machine
beeps. At the end of the program turn the dough out
onto a floured surface and cut it in half. Shape each
half into an oval and drop into 2 greased 1 lb loaf
pans. Cover loosely with oiled plastic wrap and let
rise in a warm place for 30–40 minutes or until almost
doubled in size. Bake in a preheated oven, 425°F, for
20–25 minutes. Turn out of the pans onto a cooling
rack to cool.

yogurt, honey, & fennel seed bread

Makes **1 extra-large loaf**
Time **3–4 hours**, depending
   on machine

¾ cup **water**
⅔ cup **Greek** or **whole milk
   yogurt**
4 tablespoons **honey**
2 tablespoons **unsalted
   butter**, softened
½ teaspoon **salt**
2 tablespoons **fennel seeds**,
   roughly crushed
3 cups plus 2 tablespoons
   white bread flour
1¼ teaspoons **instant yeast**

Lift the bread pan out of the machine and fit the blade.
Put the ingredients in the pan, following the order
specified in the manual.

Fit the pan into the machine and close the lid. Set to
the 2 lb loaf size on the basic white program. Select
your preferred crust setting.

At the end of the program lift the pan out of the
machine, loosen the bread with a spatula if necessary,
and shake it out onto a cooling rack to cool.

For panzanella salad, to make using the bread,
roast 4 seeded and roughly sliced sweet peppers
in a dash of olive oil until they are beginning to brown.
Tear 3½ oz bread into bite-size pieces and sprinkle
them on a foil-lined baking sheet. Drizzle with another
2 tablespoons oil and broil until browned. Quarter
1½ lb well-flavored tomatoes and scoop the seeds
into a sieve placed over a bowl. Press the seeds and
pulp in the sieve to extract the juice. Put the tomatoes,
peppers, bread, a handful of basil leaves, a finely
chopped shallot, and plenty of black olives into a
salad bowl. Beat the tomato juice with 1 crushed
garlic clove, 4 teaspoons wine vinegar, and plenty
of seasoning. Pour the dressing over the salad
and mix well.

cranberry & pomegranate bread

Makes **1 large loaf**
Time **3–4 hours**, depending
  on machine

1⅓ cups **water**
2 tablespoons **olive oil**
1 teaspoon **salt**
3 tablespoons **dried**
  pomegranate seeds
1 cup **buckwheat flour**, plus
  extra for dusting
2⅓ cups **white bread flour**
1 tablespoon **light brown**
  sugar
1¼ teaspoons **instant yeast**
⅔ cup **dried cranberries**

Lift the bread pan out of the machine and fit the blade.
Put the ingredients, except the dried cranberries, in the
pan, following the order specified in the manual.

Fit the pan into the machine and close the lid. Set to
a 1½ lb loaf size on the basic white program. Select
your preferred crust setting. Add the dried cranberries
when the machine beeps.

At the end of the program lift the pan out of the
machine and shake the bread out onto a cooling rack.
Dust the top lightly with a little extra buckwheat flour
and allow to cool. Slice and serve with cream cheese
and fruit compote, if desired.

For buckwheat, flax seed, & apricot bread, lightly
crush 4 tablespoons flax seeds using a coffee grinder
reserved for crushing seeds and spices (or use the
small bowl of a food processor). Make the bread as
above, adding ½ teaspoon cinnamon with the flour.
Use the flax seeds instead of the pomegranate seeds
and ⅔ cup chopped dried apricots instead of the
cranberries.

savory
breads

mushroom & mozzarella stromboli

Makes **1 loaf**
(about 8 thick slices)
Time **1½–2½ hours**, depending
on machine, plus shaping,
rising, and baking

Dough
1 cup **water**
3 tablespoons extra virgin
olive oil
1 teaspoon **salt**
2½ cups **white bread flour**
1 teaspoon **instant yeast**

To finish
8 oz **chestnut mushrooms**,
thinly sliced
3 tablespoons extra virgin
olive oil
10 oz **mozzarella cheese**,
sliced
½ cup **basil leaves**
2 teaspoons **green**
peppercorns in brine, rinsed
and drained
sea salt, for sprinkling

Lift the bread pan out of the machine and fit the blade. Put the dough ingredients in the pan, following the order specified in the manual. Fit the pan into the machine and close the lid. Set to the dough program.

Meanwhile, fry the mushrooms in 2 tablespoons oil until golden. Allow to cool.

At the end of the program turn the dough out onto a floured surface and roll it out to a 13 inch square. Arrange the mozzarella slices, basil leaves, and mushrooms over the dough. Lightly crush the peppercorns and sprinkle over the filling with a little salt.

Loosely roll up the dough and transfer to a large, greased baking sheet with the join underneath. Pinch the ends together to seal. Cover loosely with oiled plastic wrap and leave in a warm place for 30 minutes.

Flour a large skewer or meat fork and pierce the dough all over, making sure you go right through to the baking sheet. Drizzle with the remaining oil and sprinkle with sea salt. Bake in a preheated oven, 425°F, for about 25 minutes until risen and golden. Serve warm or cold.

For artichoke & Gruyère stromboli, make the dough as above. Drain 9 oz artichokes in olive oil and roughly chop. Roll out the dough as above and sprinkle with 1¾ cups grated Gruyère cheese, the artichokes, 6 tablespoons chopped parsley, 2 finely chopped garlic cloves, the grated zest of 1 lemon, and seasoning. Finish as above.

sweet dill & mustard loaf

Makes **1 large loaf**

Time **3–4 hours**, depending
on machine

¾ cup **water**

⅔ cup **sour cream**

3 tablespoons **grainy
mustard**

½ cup chopped **dill weed**,

1 teaspoon **salt**

3 cups plus 2 tablespoons
white bread flour

2 tablespoons **superfine
sugar**

1¼ teaspoons **instant yeast**

Lift the bread pan out of the machine and fit the blade.
Put the ingredients in the pan, following the order
specified in the manual. Add the mustard and dill with
the liquids.

Fit the pan into the machine and close the lid. Set to a
1½ lb loaf size on the basic white program. Select your
preferred crust setting.

At the end of the program lift the pan out of the
machine and shake the bread out onto a cooling rack
to cool.

For creamy smoked salmon pâté, to serve with
the freshly baked bread, roughly chop 7 oz smoked
salmon trimmings and put in a food processor. Add 2
tablespoons butter, melted and cooled, 1 tablespoon
lemon juice, 6 tablespoons cream cheese, and plenty
of black pepper. Blend until smooth, scraping down
any pieces that cling to the sides of the bowl. Transfer
to a small serving dish and chill until ready to serve.

chili & smoked paprika bread

Makes **1 large loaf**

Time **3–4 hours**, depending on machine

1 cup plus 2 tablespoons **water**

2 tablespoons **olive oil**

1 teaspoon **salt**

1 teaspoon **smoked paprika**

1 large mild fresh **red chili**, halved, seeded, and finely chopped

2 cups **white bread flour**

1 cup **whole-wheat flour**

1 teaspoon **superfine sugar**

1¼ teaspoons **instant yeast**

⅔ cup **sundried tomatoes** in oil, drained and roughly chopped (optional)

Lift the bread pan out of the machine and fit the blade. Put the ingredients, except the sundried tomatoes, in the pan following the order specified in the manual.

Fit the pan into the machine and close the lid. Set to a 1½ lb loaf size on the basic white program. Select your preferred crust setting. Add the sundried tomatoes (if using) when the machine beeps.

At the end of the program lift the pan out of the machine and shake the bread out onto a cooling rack to cool.

For spicy peanut & chili loaf, omit the smoked paprika and sundried tomatoes from the recipe. Use sesame oil instead of olive oil and add ⅓ cup crunchy peanut butter and ¼ cup grated firm creamed coconut. Add 2 finely chopped scallions when the machine beeps. Just before baking begins brush the top of the dough with milk and sprinkle with mild chili powder. Close the lid gently and complete the program.

spicy slipper breads

Makes **4 loaves**

Time **1½–2½ hours**, depending on machine, plus shaping, rising, and baking

Dough

¾ cup **water**

3 tablespoons **olive oil**

1 teaspoon **salt**

1 tablespoon **cumin seeds**, lightly crushed

1 teaspoon **ground cinnamon**

2 cups **white bread flour**

⅔ cup **chickpea flour**

1 tablespoon **superfine sugar**

1¼ teaspoons **instant yeast**

To finish

5 tablespoons **olive oil**

2 **onions**, thinly sliced

3 **garlic cloves**, crushed

13 oz can **chickpeas**, rinsed and drained

1 tablespoon chopped **mint**

4 tablespoons chopped **cilantro**

1 tablespoon **lemon juice**

8 oz **haloumi cheese**, diced

salt and **black pepper**

Lift the bread pan out of the machine and fit the blade. Put the dough ingredients in the pan, following the order specified in the manual. Add the seeds with the flours. Fit the pan into the machine and close the lid. Set to the dough program.

Heat 3 tablespoons olive oil in a pan and fry the onions for 10 minutes. Add the garlic, then the chickpeas, mint, cilantro, lemon juice, and seasoning.

At the end of the program turn the dough out onto a floured surface and divide it into 4 pieces. Roll each into an oval, about 8½ x 6½ inches, and place on a large, greased baking sheet. Stir the cheese into the chickpea mixture and sprinkle over the dough. Fold the dough over the filling so the filling is still visible. Cover with oiled plastic wrap and leave in a warm place to rise for 30 minutes or until it is half as big again.

Lightly score the dough with a floured knife and drizzle with the remaining olive oil. Sprinkle with salt and bake in a preheated oven, 425°F, for about 20 minutes until slightly risen and golden. Serve warm.

For spicy chickpea & onion loaf, fry 1 finely chopped small red onion in 1 tablespoon olive oil with 1 tablespoon lightly crushed cumin seeds and 1 teaspoon ground cinnamon. Put in the bread pan with ¾ cup water, 3 tablespoons olive oil, 1 teaspoon salt, 2 cups white bread flour, ⅔ cup chickpea flour, 1 tablespoon superfine sugar, and 1 teaspoon instant yeast, in the order given in the manual. (Add the onions with the liquids.) Set to a 1½ lb loaf size on the basic white program.

fennel, bacon, & gruyère twist

Makes **1 large loaf** (about
   8 thick slices)
Time **1½–2½ hours**, depending
   on machine, plus shaping,
   rising, and baking

Dough

¾ cup **milk**

2 **garlic cloves**, crushed

¼ cup **unsalted butter**,
   softened

1 teaspoon **salt**

2¼ cups **white bread flour**

1 teaspoon **superfine sugar**

1 teaspoon **instant yeast**

To finish

2 tablespoons **olive oil**

4 oz **bacon**, chopped

1 **fennel bulb**, chopped

2 teaspoons **fennel seeds**,
   lightly crushed, plus extra for
   sprinkling

6 oz **Gruyère cheese**, grated

black pepper

Lift the bread pan from the machine and fit the blade.
Put the dough ingredients in the pan, following the order
specified in the manual. Add the garlic with the milk.

Fit the pan into the machine and close the lid. Set to
the dough program.

Heat the oil in a skillet and gently fry the bacon, fennel,
and fennel seeds for 10 minutes until softened and
golden. Allow to cool.

At the end of the program turn the dough out onto
a floured surface and roll it out to a rectangle, about
15 x 12 inches. Sprinkle the bacon and fennel mixture
over the dough to about ¾ inch from the edges.
Sprinkle all but 2 tablespoons of the Gruyère on
top and season with plenty of pepper.

Loosely roll up the dough, starting from a short side,
and place on a large, greased baking sheet with the
join underneath. Lift one end and twist the dough to
create a corkscrew effect. Repeat at the other end.
Cover with oiled plastic wrap and let rise in a warm
place until nearly doubled in size.

Sprinkle the remaining cheese on top and sprinkle
with extra seeds. Bake in a preheated oven, 425°F,
for 25 minutes until risen and golden.

For tapenade & tomato twist, make the dough as
above, adding 2 teaspoons chopped thyme. Spread
the dough with 6 tablespoons black olive tapenade
and sprinkle with 7 oz halved cherry tomatoes.
Season with plenty of black pepper, then roll up
and finish as above.

chili chocolate bread

Makes **1 large loaf**

Time **3–4 hours**, depending on machine

1 cup **water**

3 tablespoons **sunflower oil**

1½ teaspoons **salt**

1½ teaspoons **dried red pepper flakes**

½ teaspoon **ground cinnamon**

3 oz **bittersweet chocolate** (85% cocoa solids), grated

1 tablespoon **cocoa powder**

2¼ cups **white bread flour**

⅓ cup **cornmeal**

2 tablespoons **molasses sugar**

1 teaspoon **instant yeast**

Lift the bread pan out of the machine and fit the blade. Put the ingredients in the pan, following the order specified in the manual. Add the spices, grated chocolate, and cocoa powder with the flour.

Fit the pan into the machine and close the lid. Set to a 1½ lb loaf size on the basic white program. Select your preferred crust setting.

At the end of the program lift the pan out of the machine and shake the bread out onto a cooling rack to cool.

For spicy chicken mole with chili bread, make the bread as above, omitting the chocolate and cocoa powder and adding an extra 2 tablespoons white bread flour. Allow to cool. Dust 4 halved chicken legs with 1 tablespoon lightly crushed cumin seeds and seasoning. Fry in 2 tablespoons vegetable oil in a flameproof casserole until golden. Add 1 large chopped onion and 2 crushed garlic cloves and fry for an additional 5 minutes. In a food processor blend ¼ cup blanched almonds with 2 tablespoons sesame seeds and ½ oz crumbled white bread until ground. Add 1¾ cups hot chicken stock and add to the chicken with ½ oz bittersweet chocolate, a handful of chopped fresh cilantro, and seasoning. Bring to a boil, cover with a lid, and cook in a preheated oven, 400°F, for 50 minutes. Serve slices of the chili bread with the mole.

Bread Machine

Favorite Mill.

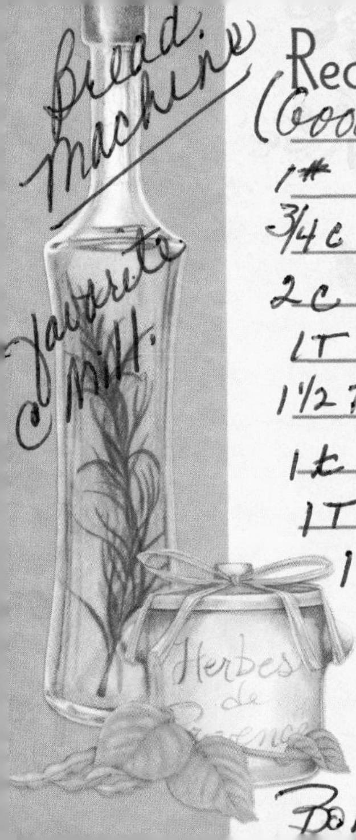

Recipe for: Country Crust White Bread
(Good for Sandwiches & toast) (airy)

1#	Ingred:	1½#
¾c	Water	1⅛ c
2c	Unbl. White Flr	3 c
1T	Dry Milk Pwd	1½ T
1½ t	Sugar	2 T
1t	Salt	1½ t
1T	Butter	2T
1½t	Yeast	3t

Serves: ________

Bob's Red Mill Flour

Add: All ingredients in order suggested by your bread machine & process on the basic bread cycle.

Net 10g col jar 15 mN
B/1
firing

olive oil, rosemary, & raisin bread

Makes **1 large loaf**

Time **1½–2½ hours**, depending on machine, plus shaping, rising, and baking

1⅓ cups **water**
6 tablespoons extra virgin **olive oil**
2 teaspoons **sea salt**, plus extra for sprinkling
2 tablespoons **milk powder**
2 teaspoons **fennel seeds**, lightly crushed
1 tablespoon chopped **rosemary**
3¾ cups **white bread flour**
1 tablespoon **superfine sugar**
2 teaspoons **instant yeast**
⅔ cup **raisins**
rosemary sprigs, to garnish

Lift the bread pan out of the machine and fit the blade. Put the ingredients, except the raisins, in the pan, following the order specified in the manual. Add the seeds and rosemary with the flour.

Fit the pan into the machine and close the lid. Set to the dough program, adding the raisins when the machine beeps.

At the end of the program turn the dough out onto a floured surface and shape it into a round. Make a hole through the center of the loaf with your fingertips, then enlarge it with your hand until the dough is ring-shaped with a hole 4 inches in diameter in the middle. Put the dough on a large, greased baking sheet, cover loosely with oiled plastic wrap and let rise in a warm place for about 45 minutes or until it has almost doubled in size.

Score the dough at intervals with a floured knife and sprinkle with rosemary sprigs and sea salt. Bake in a preheated oven, 425°F, for 40 minutes until risen and golden. Cover the bread with foil and replace the rosemary sprigs if they start to over-brown.

For Mediterranean herb bread, make the dough as above using 2 teaspoons dried oregano instead of the rosemary and omitting the raisins. Add ½ cup torn basil leaves and 3 tablespoons capers, drained and dried, when the machine beeps. Finish as above, without the rosemary sprigs.

beer & brown sugar bread

Makes **1 large loaf**

Time **3½–5 hours**, depending on machine

Dough

¾ cup **Guinness** or **English beer**

6 ablespoons cold **water**

2 tablespoons **sunflower oil**

1 teaspoon **salt**

⅔ cup **rye flour**

2¼ cups **multigrain flour**

2 tablespoons **dark brown sugar**

1¼ teaspoons **instant yeast**

To finish

1 tablespoon **milk**, to brush

1 tablespoon **poppy seeds**, for sprinkling

Lift the bread pan out of the machine and fit the blade. Put the dough ingredients in the pan, following the order specified in the manual.

Fit the pan into the machine and close the lid. Set to a 1½ lb loaf size on the whole-wheat program. Select your preferred crust setting.

Just before baking begins brush the top of the dough with the milk and sprinkle with the poppy seeds. Close the lid gently.

At the end of the program lift the pan out of the machine and shake the bread out onto a cooling rack to cool. Serve with potted cheese (see below), sliced apple, and grapes, if desired.

For potted cheese, to serve with the bread, crumble 7 oz sharp cheddar or Stilton cheese into a food processor and add ¼ cup softened butter, plenty of freshly grated nutmeg, and ½ teaspoon English mustard. Blend lightly. Add 2 tablespoons snipped chives and blend lightly to mix. Pack into a small serving dish and chill until ready to serve. If desired, seal the cheese with clarified butter to stop it drying out. Melt ¼ cup butter in a small saucepan and let the butter stand for a couple of minutes so the sediment settles on the base. Spoon the clear butter over the cheese and chill.

onion & tomato schiacciata

Makes **1 round loaf**

Time **about 1½–2½ hours**, depending on machine, plus shaping, rising, and baking

Dough

1 cup plus 2 tablespoons **water**

3 tablespoons **olive oil**

1 teaspoon **salt**

3 cups **white bread flour**

2 teaspoons **superfine sugar**

1½ teaspoons **instant yeast**

To finish

4 tablespoons **olive oil**

1 large **red onion**, thinly sliced

2 **garlic cloves**, finely chopped

1 teaspoon **superfine sugar**

3 teaspoons **black olive pesto** or **sundried tomato pesto**

⅔ cup **sundried tomatoes**, drained and sliced

small bunch of **basil**

coarse salt flakes

Lift the bread pan out of the machine and fit the blade. Put the dough ingredients in the pan, following the order specified in the manual. Fit the pan into the machine and close the lid. Set to the dough program.

Heat 1 tablespoon oil in a skillet. Add the onion and garlic and fry gently for 5 minutes until softened. Scoop out one-quarter and reserve for the topping. Add the sugar to the remaining onions and cook for a few minutes more until caramelized.

At the end of the program turn the dough out onto a floured surface and cut it in half. Roll one half to a 9 inch round. Place on an oiled baking sheet. Spread with the pesto. Top with the caramelized onions, three-quarters of the sundried tomatoes, half the basil leaves, and drizzle with 2 tablespoons oil.

Roll out the remaining dough to a circle and cover the first circle. Sprinkle with the remaining onions, tomatoes, basil leaves, and a little salt. Cover loosely with oiled plastic wrap and let rise in a warm place for 30 minutes.

Bake in a preheated oven, 400°F, for 25 minutes until golden brown and the center is cooked through. Transfer to a cutting board, drizzle with the remaining oil, and serve warm, cut into wedges.

For homemade sundried tomato pesto, drain the oil from 1 cup sundried tomatoes and finely chop in a food processor with 3 tablespoons pine nuts, 10 chopped black olives, and 2 chopped garlic cloves. Add 5 tablespoons olive oil and ¼ cup grated Parmesan cheese. Season lightly.

irish black bread

Makes **1 large loaf**

Time **3–4 hours**, depending on machine

1¼ cups **Guinness** or **stout**

2 tablespoons **unsalted butter**, softened

1½ teaspoons **salt**

2 teaspoons **ground ginger**

1¾ cups **white bread flour**

1 cup **whole-wheat flour**

3 tablespoons **molasses sugar**

1¼ teaspoons **instant yeast**

Measure the Guinness into a measuring cup and allow it to settle so that you can accurately gauge the level.

Lift the bread pan out of the machine and fit the blade. Put the ingredients in the pan, following the order specified in the manual. Add the ginger with the flour.

Fit the pan into the machine and close the lid. Set to a 1½ lb loaf size on the basic white program. Select your preferred crust setting.

At the end of the program lift the pan out of the machine and shake the bread out onto a cooling rack to cool.

olive & tomato bread

Makes **1 large loaf**

Time **1½–2½ hours**, depending on machine, plus shaping, rising, and baking

Dough

1 cup plus 2 tablespoons **water**

2 tablespoons **olive oil**

1 teaspoon **salt**

3 cups **white bread flour**

1 teaspoon **superfine sugar**

1¼ teaspoons **instant yeast**

To finish

⅔ cup pitted or stuffed **green olives**, roughly chopped

15 **sundried tomatoes** (not in oil), roughly chopped

coarse sea salt and **paprika**, for sprinkling

Lift the bread pan out of the machine and fit the blade. Put the dough ingredients in the pan, following the order specified in the manual.

Fit the pan into the machine and close the lid. Set to the dough program.

At the end of the program lift the pan out of the machine and turn the dough out onto a floured surface. Gradually work in the chopped olives and tomatoes. Pat the dough into a circle about 8 inches across and use a floured knife to mark it into 8 wedges. Do not cut right through to the base.

Sprinkle the salt and paprika over the dough, transfer to a large, lightly greased backing sheet, cover loosely with oiled plastic wrap and let rise in a warm place for 30 minutes until it is half as big again.

Bake in a preheated oven, 400°F, for 30 minutes. Check after 15 minutes and cover with foil if over-browning. Transfer to a cooling rack to cool.

For pancetta & Parmesan bread, finely chop 4 oz pancetta. Heat 1 tablespoon olive oil in a small skillet and fry the pancetta with 1 chopped shallot for 5 minutes until it is beginning to brown. Allow to cool. Make the bread as above, adding the pancetta and shallot and ½ cup grated Parmesan cheese to the dough instead of the olives and tomatoes. Finish as above.

pissaladière

Makes **1 large tart**

Time **1½–2½ hours**, depending on machine, plus shaping, rising, and baking

Dough

1 large **egg**, beaten
1 tablespoon **olive oil**
½ teaspoon **salt**
1½ cups **white bread flour**
1 tablespoon **superfine sugar**
¾ teaspoon **instant yeast**

To finish

4 tablespoons extra virgin **olive oil**
1¼ lb **onions**, thinly sliced
2 teaspoons chopped **thyme**
2 oz can **anchovies** in olive oil
about 10 pitted **black olives**
salt and **black pepper**
thyme sprigs, to garnish

Lift the bread pan out of the machine and fit the blade. Put the egg in a measuring cup and make it up to ⅔ cup with water. Put the dough ingredients in the pan, following the order specified in the manual. Fit the pan into the machine and close the lid. Set to the dough program. Check the dough after 5 minutes' kneading and add 1 tablespoon more water if it feels dry.

Prepare the topping. Heat 2 tablespoons oil in a skillet and fry the onions for about 20 minutes, stirring frequently. Stir in the thyme and plenty of seasoning.

At the end of the program turn the dough out onto a floured surface and roll it out thinly to a circle about 13 inches across. Lift it onto a large, greased baking sheet, reshape the circle, and make a rim by folding over the edges of the dough and pressing them down firmly. Let stand, uncovered, for 10 minutes.

Bake in a preheated oven, 425°F, for 5 minutes. Spread with the onion mixture in an even layer. Drain the can of anchovies, reserving the oil. Cut the anchovies into thin strips and use them to make a lattice pattern over the dough. Place the olives in the spaces between the anchovies. Drizzle with the anchovy oil and remaining olive oil.

Return the tart to the oven for 10–15 minutes until golden. Serve warm, sprinkled with extra thyme sprigs.

For pesto & mushroom tart, make the dough as above, roll out, and spread with 5 tablespoons pesto. Fry 10 oz sliced mushrooms in 3 tablespoons oil. Sprinkle over the pesto and finish as above.

minted zucchini & lemon loaf

Makes **1 large loaf**
Time **3–4 hours**, depending
on machine, plus standing

1 large **zucchini**, about
8 oz
2 tablespoons **salt**, plus
½ teaspoon
¾ cup **water**
5 tablespoons **olive oil**
½ teaspoon freshly ground
black pepper
grated zest of 1 **lemon**
2 tablespoons chopped **mint**
3 tablespoons **capers**, rinsed
and drained
2½ cups **white bread flour**
1 tablespoon **superfine sugar**
1¼ teaspoons **instant yeast**

Coarsely grate the zucchini and mix in a colander with
2 tablespoons salt. Let stand for 30 minutes. Rinse the
zucchini in plenty of cold water and pat dry between
several layers of paper towel.

Lift the bread pan out of the machine and fit the blade.
Put the ingredients in the pan, following the order
specified in the manual.

Fit the pan into the machine and close the lid. Set to a
1½ lb loaf size on the basic white program. Select your
preferred crust setting. Add the zucchini, lemon, mint,
and capers when the machine beeps.

At the end of the program lift the pan out of the
machine and shake the bread out onto a cooling rack
to cool.

For feta & yogurt dip, to serve with the toasted
bread, beat ⅔ cup Greek or whole milk yogurt in a
bowl with ⅔ cup mayonnaise. Stir in 2 tablespoons
snipped chives and 2 tablespoons chopped parsley.
Crumble 4 oz feta into the mixture and mix well.
Season with salt and pepper. Turn into a small serving
dish, cover, and chill until ready to serve.

spinach & manchego ring loaf

Makes **1 large ring loaf**
(about 10 thick slices)
Time **1½–2½ hours**, depending
on machine, plus cooking,
shaping, rising, and baking

Dough

2 tablespoons **olive oil**
1 small **onion**, finely chopped
1 cup **water**
¼ cup grated **Parmesan
cheese**, plus extra for
sprinkling
1 teaspoon **salt**
2¾ cups **white bread flour**
1 tablespoon **superfine sugar**
1½ teaspoons **instant yeast**

To finish

3½ cups young **spinach
leaves**
7 oz **Manchego cheese**, cut
into small dice
½ teaspoon freshly grated
nutmeg
2 **garlic cloves**, finely chopped
⅓ cup **raisins**
⅓ cup **pine nuts**,
lightly toasted
beaten **egg**, to glaze
salt and **black pepper**

Heat the oil in a skillet and gently fry the onion until softened. Allow to cool.

Lift the bread pan out of the machine and fit the blade. Put the dough ingredients in the pan, following the order specified in the manual. Add the onion and cheese with the water. Fit the pan into the machine and close the lid. Set to the dough program.

Put the spinach in a saucepan with 1 tablespoon water and cover with a lid. Heat gently until the spinach has wilted. Drain and pat the spinach dry between layers of paper towel. In a bowl, mix together the Manchego with the nutmeg, garlic, raisins, pine nuts, and seasoning.

At the end of the program turn the dough out onto a floured surface and roll it out to a rectangle, about 15 x 12 inches. Spread the filling almost to the edges. Roll up the dough, starting from a long side. Transfer the roll to a large, greased baking sheet with the join underneath. Bend the ends round to make a ring and push the ends firmly together to seal. Cover loosely with oiled plastic wrap and leave in a warm place for about 45 minutes until risen by at least half again.

Brush the dough with beaten egg to glaze and sprinkle with extra grated Parmesan. Make vertical scores to the middle of the dough so that the filling is revealed. Bake in a preheated oven, 400°F, for 30–35 minutes until risen and golden. Serve warm or cold.

For cheddar cheese & chutney ring, make as above, filling with ¾ cup tomato chutney and 2 cups grated cheddar cheese.

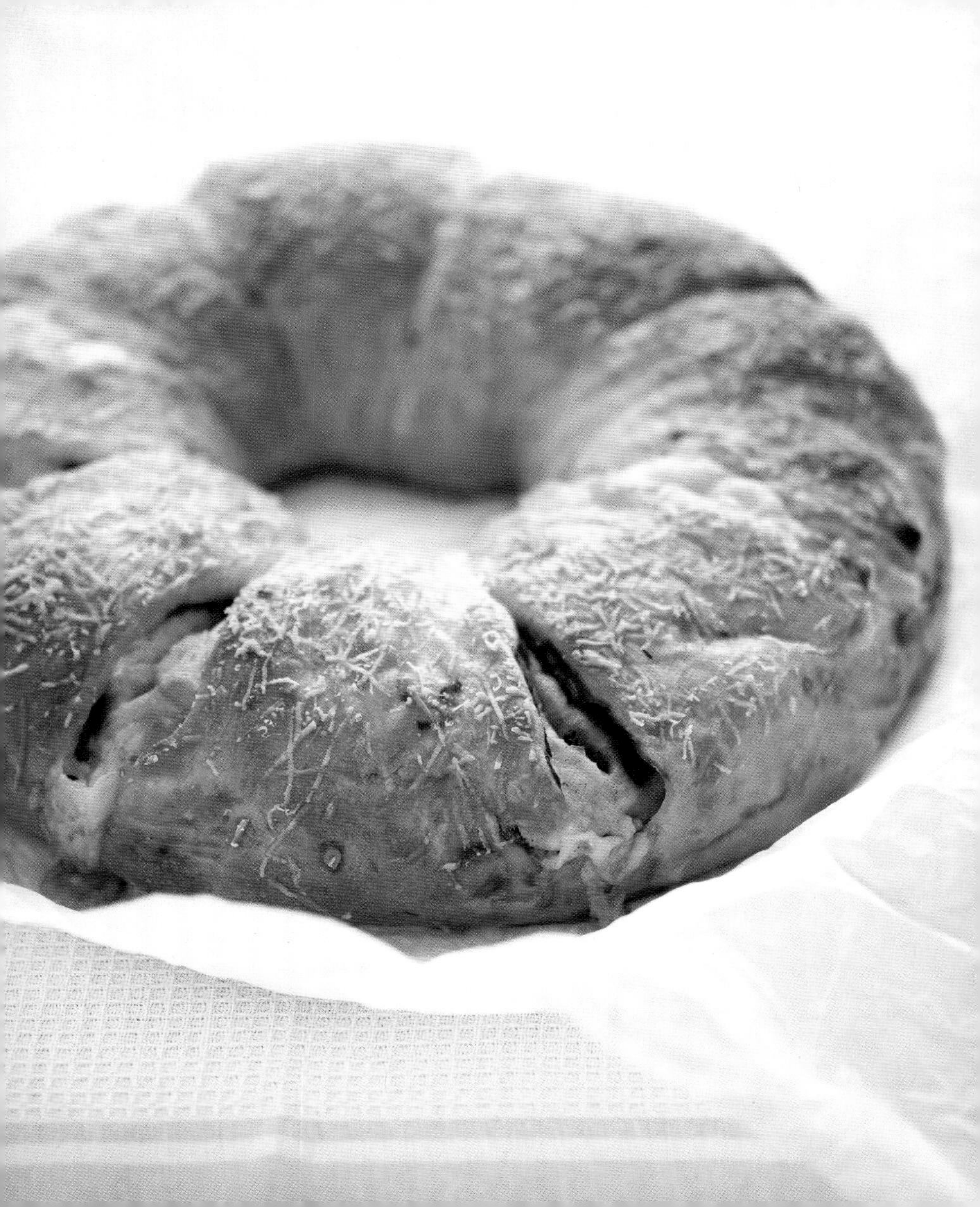

provençal-style picnic slice

Makes **10 thick slices**

Time **1½–2½ hours**, depending on machine, plus shaping, rising, and baking

Dough

2 tablespoons **olive oil**

4 tablespoons chopped **herbs**, such as thyme, oregano, and rosemary

¾ cup grated **Parmesan cheese**

1 cup **milk**

1 teaspoon **salt**

2¼ cups **white bread flour**

1 tablespoon **superfine sugar**

1 teaspoon **instant yeast**

To finish

5 tablespoons **sundried tomato paste**

12 oz **mixed roasted vegetables**, such as sweet peppers, zucchini, and red onions (see pages 230–31)

2 tablespoons **olive oil**

milk, to brush

¼ cup grated **Parmesan cheese**, for sprinkling

salt and **black pepper**

Lift the bread pan out of the machine and fit the blade. Put the dough ingredients in the pan, following the order specified in the manual. Add the herbs and cheese with the milk.

Fit the pan into the machine and close the lid. Set to the dough program.

At the end of the program turn the dough out onto a floured surface and roll it out to an 11 inch square. Spread with the tomato paste and sprinkle with the roasted vegetables. Drizzle with the oil and a little salt and pepper.

Roll up the dough so the filling is enclosed and cut it into 10 thick slices. Arrange the slices in a staggered line on a large, greased baking sheet, resting each slice against the one behind so the filling is revealed. Cover with oiled plastic wrap and let rise in a warm place for about 40 minutes or until almost doubled in size.

Brush the dough with milk and sprinkle with cheese. Bake in a preheated oven, 400°F, for 25 minutes until risen and golden. Serve warm, broken into slices.

For leek & Stilton picnic loaf, make the dough as above but reducing the Parmesan by half. Thinly slice 12 oz leeks and sauté them in 2 tablespoons butter until soft. Allow to cool. Roll out the dough as above and sprinkle with the leeks, 5 oz crumbled, creamy Stilton cheese, and plenty of black pepper. Roll up the dough and finish as above.

pancetta & artichoke pizza

Serves **4**

Time **1½–2½ hours**, depending
on machine, plus shaping,
rising, and baking

Dough

¾ cup **water**

2 tablespoons **olive oil**

1 teaspoon **salt**

2 cups **white bread flour**

1 teaspoon **superfine sugar**

1 teaspoon **instant yeast**

To finish

9 oz jar **artichokes** in olive oil

4 oz sliced **pancetta**, cut into
large pieces

5 tablespoons **pesto**

4 tablespoons **pine nuts**

3 oz piece **Pecorino cheese**
or **Parmesan cheese**, to
serve

black pepper

Lift the bread pan out of the machine and fit the blade.
Put the dough ingredients in the pan, following the
order specified in the manual.

Fit the pan into the machine and close the lid. Set to
the dough program.

Drain the artichokes, reserving 2 tablespoons of the
oil, and slice them into smaller pieces. Heat the
reserved oil in a skillet and fry the pancetta until it just
starts to brown.

At the end of the program turn the dough out onto a
floured surface and roll it out to a circle 12 inches
across. Transfer to a large, greased baking sheet and
spread to ½ inch of the edges with the pesto. Sprinkle
with the artichokes, then the pancetta, pine nuts, and
plenty of black pepper.

Bake in a preheated oven, 400°F, for about 15 minutes
until the crust is pale golden. Shave plenty of cheese
over the top to serve.

For goats' cheese & onion pizzas, fry 1 lb sliced red
onions in 3 tablespoons olive oil until softened. Make
the dough as above and cut it into quarters. Roll out
each piece to a circle 8 inches across and transfer to
2 greased baking sheets. Sprinkle with the onions.
Thinly slice 7 oz goat cheese and arrange over the
top. Sprinkle each pizza with a few black olives and a
little of chopped oregano. Season with salt and
pepper and drizzle each with a teaspoon of olive oil.
Bake as above.

potato & thyme bread

Makes **2 small loaves**
Time **1½–2½ hours**, depending
on machine, plus cooking,
shaping, rising, and baking

1 lb well-flavored **floury
potatoes**, such as russet,
cut into ½ inch dice
¾ cup **milk**
⅓ cup **unsalted butter**,
softened
2 teaspoons **sea salt**, plus
extra for sprinkling
2 tablespoons chopped
lemon thyme
¼ teaspoon **ground turmeric**
3 cups **white bread flour**
2 teaspoons **superfine sugar**
1½ teaspoons **instant yeast**
thyme sprigs, to garnish

Cook the potatoes in boiling, salted water for
10 minutes or until tender. Drain thoroughly and return
one-third to the pan. Mash until smooth; let cool.

Lift the bread pan out of the machine and fit the blade.
Put the ingredients, except the thyme sprigs, in the
pan, following the order specified in the manual. Add
the mashed potatoes with the milk. Fit the pan into the
machine and close the lid. Set to the dough program.
Melt the remaining butter.

At the end of the program, knead in the remaining
diced potatoes. Divide the dough in half and shape into
2 long, slender loaves. Space slightly apart on a large,
greased baking sheet. Cover loosely with oiled plastic
wrap and let rise in a warm place for 45 minutes.

Brush the loaves with half the melted butter and
sprinkle with sea salt. Bake in a preheated oven, 425°F,
for 25 minutes until risen and golden. Brush with the
remaining melted butter and sprinkle with extra thyme
leaves. Serve warm or cool.

For spicy potato bread, boil and mash 7 oz potatoes
and let cool. Chop 4 oz bacon and fry in a dash of
oil. Put ¾ cup milk, 1 teaspoon salt, 2 tablespoons
curry paste, 2 tablespoons soft butter, ¾ cup chopped
cilantro, 3 cups white bread flour, 2 teaspoons
superfine sugar, and 1½ teaspoons instant yeast in the
bread pan following the order specified in the manual.
Add the potatoes with the milk. Set to a 1½ lb loaf size
on the basic white program. Add the bacon when the
machine beeps.

sweet potato & tarragon bread

Makes **1 large loaf**

Time **3–4 hours**, depending
on machine, plus cooking

7 oz **sweet potatoes**

¾ cup **milk**

¼ cup **unsalted butter**,
softened

2 teaspoons **salt**

2 teaspoons **Dijon mustard**

4 tablespoons **mustard seeds**

2 cups **white bread flour**

1 cup **whole-wheat flour** or
multigrain flour

1 teaspoon **superfine sugar**

1¼ teaspoons **instant yeast**

4 oz firm **goat cheese**, diced

2 tablespoons **tarragon**,
leaves pulled from stalks

Peel and dice the sweet potatoes and cook them in boiling water for about 10 minutes until just tender. Drain thoroughly, return to the saucepan, and mash until smooth. Allow to cool.

Lift the bread pan out of the machine and fit the blade. Put the ingredients, except the cheese and tarragon, in the pan, following the order specified in the manual. Add the mashed potatoes with the milk.

Fit the pan into the machine and close the lid. Set to a 1½ lb loaf size on the basic white program. Select your preferred crust setting. Add the cheese and tarragon when the machine beeps.

At the end of the program lift the pan out of the machine and shake the bread out onto a cooling rack to cool.

For seeded pumpkin bread with cajun spices, peel, seed, and dice 7 oz pumpkin and cook in boiling water until only just tender. Drain thoroughly and mash. Put ¾ cup milk, ¼ cup soft butter, 2 teaspoons salt, 2 tablespoons Cajun spice blend, 3 cups white bread flour, 1 teaspoon sugar, and 1½ teaspoons instant yeast in the bread pan, following the order specified in the manual. (Add the pumpkin mash with the milk and spice blend with the flour.) Add 5 tablespoons pumpkin seeds when the machine beeps. After baking shake the bread out onto a cooling rack to cool.

onion & red leicester bread

Makes **1 large loaf**
Time **3–4 hours**, depending
 on machine

1 tablespoon **olive oil**
1 **red onion**, thinly sliced
3 teaspoons **superfine sugar**
1 cup **water**
4 oz **red Leicester cheese**,
 grated
1 teaspoon **salt**
1 teaspoon **ready-made** or
 powdered English mustard
½ teaspoon **peppercorns**,
 roughly crushed
2½ cups plus 2 tablespoons
 white bread flour
1¼ teaspoons **instant yeast**

Lift the bread pan out of the machine and fit the blade.
Put the ingredients, except the olive oil, onion, and sugar,
in the pan, following the order given in the manual.

Fit the pan into the machine and close the lid. Set to
a 1½ lb loaf size on the basic white program with a
pale crust setting. (If your machine does not have a
setting for crust color, set the machine to sweet bread
to prevent the cheese over-darkening the crust).

Heat the oil in a skillet while the program is running.
Add the onion and fry over a medium heat for
5 minutes until softened. Sprinkle with 1 teaspoon
of the sugar and fry for 5 more minutes until the onion
is lightly caramelized. Allow to cool.

Add the onions gradually when the machine beeps.

At the end of the program lift the pan out of the machine
and shake the bread onto a cooling rack to cool.

For Stilton & spinach whirl, put 1 cup plus
2 tablespoons milk, 2 tablespoons soft butter,
1 teaspoon salt, 1 teaspoon ground mace, 2½ cups
plus 2 tablespoons white bread flour, 1 teaspoon
sugar, 1¼ teaspoons instant yeast in the bread pan,
following the order specified in the manual. Set to the
dough program. Lightly wilt 2 cups washed spinach
leaves in a pan. Cool. Roll out the dough to a 10 inch
square and sprinkle with the spinach and 7 oz
crumbled Stilton. Roll up and drop into a 3 lb greased
loaf pan. Cover with oiled plastic wrap and let rise for
45 minutes. Bake in a preheated oven, 400°F, for
35–40 minutes until risen.

pesto & marinated olive bread

Makes **1 large loaf**

Time **3–4 hours**, depending on machine

¾ cup **water**

2 tablespoons **olive oil**

2 tablespoons **pesto**

1 teaspoon **salt**

2½ cups plus 2 tablespoons **white bread flour**

1 teaspoon **superfine sugar**

1¼ teaspoons **instant yeast**

⅔ cup pitted and **marinated mixed olives**, halved

Lift the bread pan out of the machine and fit the blade. Put the ingredients, except the olives, in the pan, following the order specified in the manual.

Fit the pan into the machine and close the lid. Set to a 1½ lb loaf size on the basic white program. Select your preferred crust setting.

Add the olives when the machine beeps, adding them gradually to prevent the blade jamming.

At the end of the program lift the pan out of the machine and shake the bread out onto a cooling rack to cool.

For Emmenthal & hot pepper bread, use 2 oz hot red Jalapeño chili peppers from a jar. Pat dry on paper towels and roughly chop. Make the bread as above, omitting the pesto and olives and adding the chopped chili peppers, 4 oz diced Emmenthal cheese, and ½ cup chopped parsley or cilantro when the machine beeps.

flat breads

pita bread

Makes **8 breads**

Time **1½–2½ hours**,
depending on machine, plus
shaping, rising, and baking

1 cup **water**
1 tablespoon **olive oil**
1 teaspoon **salt**
½ teaspoon **ground cumin**
2⅓ cups **white bread flour**
1 teaspoon **superfine sugar**
1 teaspoon **instant yeast**

Lift the bread pan out of the machine and fit the blade. Put the ingredients in the pan, following the order specified in the manual.

Fit the pan into the machine and close the lid. Set to the dough program.

At the end of the program turn the dough out onto a floured surface and cut it into 8 equal-size pieces. Roll out each piece to an oval about 6 inches long. Arrange in a single layer on a well-floured clean, dry dish towel. Cover loosely with a second clean, dry dish towel and let rise in a warm place for 30 minutes.

Put a floured baking sheet in a preheated oven, 450°F, and allow to heat up for 5 minutes. Transfer half the breads to the baking sheet and cook for 5–6 minutes until just beginning to brown. Remove from the oven and allow to cool on a cooling rack while you cook the remainder. Wrap the still warm pitas in a clean, dry dish towel to keep them soft until ready to serve. If they are left to go cold, warm the pitas through in a hot oven before serving.

For olive & herb mini pitas, make the dough as above, but add ⅓ cup pitted and chopped black olives and a large handful of chopped parsley and mint to the dough when the machine beeps. At the end of the program turn the dough out onto a floured surface and cut it into 16 pieces. Thinly roll out each piece to an oval 4–5 inches long. Let rise and bake as above.

tomato focaccia

Makes **2 loaves**
Time **1½–2½ hours**,
  depending on machine, plus
  shaping, rising, and baking

Dough
3 cups **white bread flour**
1 teaspoon **superfine sugar**
1 teaspoon **salt**
1½ teaspoons **instant yeast**
3 tablespoons **olive oil**
1 cup plus 2 tablespoons
  water

To finish
7 oz **cherry tomatoes**
a few **rosemary sprigs**
a few **black olives**
1 teaspoon **salt flakes**
3 tablespoons **olive oil**

Lift the bread pan out of the machine and fit the blade. Put the dough ingredients in the pan, following the order specified in the manual.

Fit the pan into the machine and close the lid. Set to the dough program.

At the end of the program turn the dough out onto a floured surface and cut it in half. Press each into a rough oval a little larger than your hand.

Transfer the loaves to 2 greased baking sheets and use the end of a wooden spoon to make indentations over the surface. Press the tomatoes into some of the indentations, add small sprigs of rosemary and olives into some of the others. Sprinkle with salt flakes and leave, uncovered, for 20 minutes.

Drizzle the loaves with a little of the oil and bake in a preheated oven, 400°F, for 15 minutes. Swap the shelf positions during cooking so that both loaves brown evenly. Drizzle with the remaining oil and serve warm or cold, torn into pieces.

For onion, sage, & gorgonzola focaccia, make the dough as above, adding 1 tablespoon chopped sage with the flour. After shaping and making indentations, sprinkle the loaves with ½ small red onion, very finely sliced, and 3 oz crumbled Gorgonzola. Drizzle with olive oil as above and sprinkle with small sage leaves halfway through baking.

94

semolina & olive oil bread

Makes **6 breads**

Time **1½–2½ hours**,
   depending on machine, plus
   shaping, rising, and baking

¾ cup **water**
6 tablespoons **olive oil**
2 teaspoons **salt**
1¼ cups **white bread flour**
1¼ cups fine **semolina**, plus
   extra for sprinkling
1 teaspoon **instant yeast**

Lift the bread pan out of the machine and fit the blade. Put the ingredients in the pan, following the order specified in the manual.

Fit the pan into the machine and close the lid. Set to the dough program.

At the end of the program turn the dough out onto a floured surface and divide it into 6 equal pieces. Shape each into a ball and roll it out until about 6 inches in diameter.

Grease a large baking sheet and dust it with semolina. Space the breads about ¾ inch apart on the baking sheet and sprinkle with extra semolina. Press the semolina down gently. Cover loosely with oiled plastic wrap and let rise in a warm place for 30 minutes.

Bake in a preheated oven, 425°F, for 12–15 minutes until golden. Transfer to a cooling rack to cool.

For chorizo & fava bean tostadas, make the bread as above and cool. Cut 10 oz piece chorizo sausage into ½ inch dice. Cook 1¼ cups baby fava beans in boiling water for 3 minutes. Drain and cool, then pop the beans out of their skins into a bowl. Heat 4 tablespoons extra virgin olive oil in a skillet and gently fry the chorizo and 2 thinly sliced shallots for 5 minutes, stirring. Toss with the beans, 2 teaspoons lemon juice, and a little salt and pepper. Place each bread under a medium grill until toasted. Serve topped with the warm or cold chorizo and fava bean mix.

piadina

Makes **8 breads**

Time **1½−2½ hours**,
depending on machine, plus
shaping, rising, and baking

1¼ cups **water**

2 tablespoons **lard**, melted

2 teaspoons **salt**

2 teaspoons **fennel seeds**,
crushed

2¾ cups **white bread flour**

1 teaspoon **superfine sugar**

1¼ teaspoons **instant yeast**

Lift the bread pan out of the machine and fit the blade.
Put the ingredients in the pan, following the order
specified in the manual.

Fit the pan into the machine and close the lid. Set to
the dough program.

At the end of the program turn the dough out onto a
floured surface and divide it into 8 equal pieces. Roll
out each piece to a circle 9 inches across. Leave the
rounds on the floured surface, covered with a clean, dry
dish towel for 15 minutes.

Heat a large skillet or griddle until very hot then reduce
to the lowest setting. Place a piece of dough in the pan
and cook for 5−6 minutes until golden brown. Pierce
any large bubbles that form with a fork and turn the
bread several times so that it doesn't start to catch.

Slide the piadina onto a tray or plate and keep covered
with a clean, damp dish towel to keep the bread soft
and warm while you cook the remainder.

For Italian wraps with mozzarella & cured meats,
spread a hot piadina with 1−2 teaspoons pesto.
Thinly slice 3 oz mozzarella cheese and sprinkle on
top. Drizzle with a little extra virgin olive oil and plenty
of black pepper. Arrange slices of cured meat (such
as prosciutto, coppa, or salami) over the cheese.
Sprinkle with arugula leaves, if desired. Fold the
piadina into 3 to serve.

buttered garlic & basil sticks

Makes **about 20 sticks**

Time **1½–2½ hours**,
depending on machine, plus
shaping, rising, and baking

Dough

¾ cup **water**

2 tablespoons **olive oil**

1 teaspoon **salt**

2½ cups **white bread flour**

1 teaspoon **superfine sugar**

1¼ teaspoons **instant yeast**

To finish

½ cup **unsalted butter**

4 **garlic cloves**, finely
chopped

small bunch of **basil**, leaves
torn into pieces

coarse sea salt

black pepper

Lift the bread pan out of the machine and fit the blade.
Put the dough ingredients in the pan, following the
order specified in the manual. Fit the pan into the
machine and close the lid. Set to the dough program.

At the end of the program turn the dough out onto a
floured surface and cut it in half. Roll each half to a
thin oval about 14 x 7 inches. Transfer to 2 greased
baking sheets and cut into 1 inch strips, making cuts a
little in from the edge of the dough so the strips are
still held together at the ends.

Sprinkle the dough with a little coarse salt. Cover
loosely with oiled plastic wrap and leave in a warm
place for 30 minutes or until the dough has risen
around the edges.

Bake in a preheated oven, 425°F, for 8–10 minutes
until the bread sounds hollow when tapped with the
fingertips. Transfer to 2 large plates.

Melt a small piece of butter in a saucepan and fry the
garlic for 2–3 minutes until beginning to brown. Add
the remaining butter, the basil leaves, and pepper to
taste. When the butter has melted, brush this over the
hot bread, separate into sticks, and serve immediately.

For cumin & cilantro sticks, make the dough as
above, adding 2 teaspoons crushed cumin seeds.
Melt 2 tablespoons butter in a saucepan and gently
fry 1 finely chopped scallion and 1 thinly sliced red
chili. Add 4 tablespoons chopped cilantro and ⅓ cup
more butter. Heat until the butter has melted, then
brush it over the hot bread.

turkish pide

Makes **4 pide**

Time **1½–2½ hours**,
   depending on machine, plus
   shaping, rising, and baking

Dough

½ cup **water**

½ cup **plain yogurt**

2 tablespoons **olive oil**

2 teaspoons **salt**

4 tablespoons **sesame seeds**

2½ cups **white bread flour**

1 teaspoon **superfine sugar**

1 teaspoon **instant yeast**

To finish

4 tablespoons **olive oil**

1 large **onion**, chopped

2 **garlic cloves**, chopped

8 oz **ground lamb**

good pinch of **saffron strands**

1 tablespoon **coriander
   seeds**, lightly crushed

⅓ cup ready-to-eat **dried
   apricots**, sliced

½ cup **pine nuts**

salt and **black pepper**

chopped **parsley**, for sprinkling

Lift the bread pan out of the machine and fit the blade. Put the dough ingredients in the pan, following the order specified in the manual. Add the sesame seeds with the flour.

Fit the pan into the machine and close the lid. Set to the dough program.

Make the topping. Heat 2 tablespoons oil in a skillet and fry the onion for 5 minutes to soften. Add the garlic and lamb and fry for 5–10 minutes until beginning to brown, breaking up the lamb with a wooden spoon. Stir in the saffron, coriander, apricots, and pine nuts and cook, stirring, for 5 minutes. Season with salt and pepper.

At the end of the program turn the dough out onto a floured surface and cut it into quarters. Roll each piece to an oval, about 8 inches long. Transfer to 2 greased baking sheets and prick the bases with a fork. Spread with the meat mixture to about ½ inch of the edges. Cover loosely with oiled plastic wrap and let rise in a warm place for 30 minutes.

Drizzle the remaining oil over the breads and bake in a preheated oven, 400°F, for about 20 minutes until golden. Serve sprinkled with parsley.

For feta & onion pide, make and shape the dough as above. Transfer to the baking sheets and prick with a fork. Sprinkle 7 oz crumbled feta cheese over the dough to ½ inch of the edges. Chop 4 scallions and lightly crush 1 teaspoon cumin seeds. Sprinkle the scallions and seeds over the feta and season with salt and pepper. Let rise as above and drizzle each pide with 1 tablespoon olive oil before cooking.

fougasse

Makes **2 loaves**

Time **1½–2½ hours**,
depending on machine, plus
shaping, rising, and baking

1 cup **water**
4 tablespoons **olive oil**, plus
extra for drizzling
1½ teaspoons **salt**
3 tablespoons fresh chopped
or 1½ teaspoons dried
mixed herbs, such as
lavender, thyme, and
rosemary
3 cups **white bread flour**
2 teaspoons **superfine sugar**
1¼ teaspoons **instant yeast**
coarse sea salt, for sprinkling

Lift the bread pan out of the machine and fit the blade.
Add the ingredients to the pan, following the order
specified in the manual.

Fit the pan into the machine and close the lid. Set to
the dough program.

At the end of the program turn the dough out onto a
floured surface and cut it in half. Roll each half to an oval
12 x 8 inches.

Transfer the dough to 2 greased baking sheets. Make
5 diagonal slits in the dough, then open out the outer
edges of the slits by lifting the edges of the bread and
widening the gap with a fingertip. Cover loosely with
oiled plastic wrap and leave in a warm place to rise for
30 minutes or until puffy.

Bake in a preheated oven, 425°F, for 8–10 minutes
until golden. Drizzle with a little olive oil and sprinkle
with a little sea salt. Transfer to a cooling rack after
10 minutes to cool completely.

For Parmesan & olive bread sticks, make the dough
as above, adding ⅓ cup black olives, finely chopped,
and ½ cup grated Parmesan cheese when the
machine beeps. Roll out the dough on a floured
surface to a rectangle, about 12 x 8 inches. Cover
loosely with a floured, clean dish towel and let stand
for 20 minutes. Cut across into long, thin strips and
space, slightly apart, on a greased and semolina-
dusted baking sheet. Brush lightly with beaten egg and
sprinkle with salt. Bake in a preheated oven, 425°F, for
15–20 minutes until golden. Cool on a cooling rack.

seeded naan breads

Makes **6 breads**
Time **1½–2½ hours**,
   depending on machine,
   plus shaping, rising,
   and cooking

12 **cardamom pods**
2 teaspoons **coriander seeds**
2 teaspoons **cumin seeds**
6 tablespoons **water**
4 tablespoons **plain yogurt**
1 tablespoon **vegetable oil**
1 teaspoon **salt**
2 teaspoons **black onion seeds**
1¾ cups **white bread flour**
1 teaspoon **superfine sugar**
¾ teaspoon **instant yeast**
2 tablespoons **butter** or **ghee**, melted

Crush the cardamom pods using a mortar and pestle to release the seeds. Discard the shells. Add the coriander and cumin seeds and grind until crushed.

Lift the bread pan out of the machine and fit the blade. Put the ingredients, except the butter or ghee, in the pan, following the order specified in the manual. Add all the seeds with the flour. Fit the pan into the machine and close the lid. Set to the dough program.

At the end of the program turn the dough out onto a floured surface and divide it into 6 pieces. Roll each out to a tear shape about 8½ inches long. Place on floured trays; dust with flour. Cover loosely with a clean, dry dish towel; let rise in a warm place for 20 minutes.

Preheat the broiler to its highest setting and heat a large baking sheet under the broiler. Brush the dough with the butter or ghee and cook on the baking sheet in 2 or 3 batches until puffy and patchily brown. Stack the cooked breads on a plate and cover with a clean, dry dish towel while you cook the remainder.

For Peshwari naan, omit the seeds. Mix together ½ cup ground almonds, ⅓ cup shredded coconut, 3 tablespoons golden raisins, and a pinch of sugar. Divide the dough into 12 pieces and roll each out to a tear shape, about 5 inches long. Dampen the edges of half the shapes with water and sprinkle the nut mixture in the center. Drizzle with 2 tablespoons melted butter. Place the remaining pieces of dough on top and re-roll so that the breads are about 8½ inches long. Brush with butter or ghee and cook as above.

asian-style flatbreads

Makes **8 breads**

Time **1½–2½ hours**,
  depending on machine,
  plus shaping, rising,
  and cooking

6 tablespoons **sesame seeds**
1 cup **water**
1 **garlic clove**, chopped
1 inch piece of **fresh ginger
  root**, grated
1 cup roughly chopped
  cilantro
2 tablespoons **sesame oil**
2 teaspoons **salt**
2¾ cups **white bread flour**
1 tablespoon **superfine sugar**
1¼ teaspoons **instant yeast**

Put the sesame seeds in a food processor and grind until broken up. (The seeds won't grind to a powder.)

Lift the bread pan out of the machine and fit the blade. Put the ingredients in the pan, following the order specified in the manual. Add the seeds, garlic, ginger, and cilantro with the water.

Fit the pan into the machine and close the lid. Set to the dough program.

At the end of the program turn the dough out onto a floured surface and divide it into 8 equal pieces. Roll out each piece to a circle 8 inches across. Leave the rounds on the floured surface, covered with a clean, dry dish towel, for 15 minutes.

Heat a large skillet or griddle, then reduce to the lowest setting. Place a piece of dough in the pan and cook for 3–4 minutes, turning once, until golden brown in places. Slide the bread onto a plate and cover with a clean, damp dish towel while you cook the rest.

For spicy chicken wraps, diagonally slice 1 bunch of scallions. Thinly slice 2 celery sticks. Heat 3 tablespoons vegetable oil in a large skillet and fry the onions and celery for 2 minutes. Drain to a plate. Add 3 thinly sliced chicken breast fillets to the pan and fry quickly, stirring, for about 5 minutes or until cooked through. Add 4 tablespoons sweet chili sauce and 2 teaspoons rice wine vinegar. Return the onions and celery to the pan and stir to mix. Spoon the filling across 4 of the wraps (the remainder can be chilled or frozen for another time) and sprinkle with pea shoots or sprouting beans. Roll up and serve warm.

spiced chickpea flatbreads

Makes **12 breads**

Time **1½–2½ hours**,
  depending on machine, plus
  shaping, rising, and baking

½ cup **tahini paste**
2 tablespoons **olive oil**
2 teaspoons **salt**
1 tablespoon **baharat spice
  blend** (see below)
3 cups **kamut flour**
2 tablespoons **light brown
  sugar**
1 teaspoon **instant yeast**

Put the tahini paste in a measuring jug and make it up to 1¼ cups with hot water. Stir until the tahini paste has softened, then leave until only just warm.

Lift the bread pan out of the machine and fit the blade. Put the ingredients in the pan, following the order specified in the manual. Add the spice with the flour.

Fit the pan into the machine and close the lid. Set to the dough program.

At the end of the program turn the dough out onto a floured surface and divide it into 12 equal pieces. Roll out each piece to an oval about 5 inches long. Arrange them in a single layer on a well-floured, clean, dry dish towel. Cover loosely with a second, clean dish towel and let rise in a warm place for 20 minutes.

Put 2 floured baking sheets in a preheated oven, 450°F, and allow to heat up for 5 minutes. Transfer the breads to the baking sheets and cook for 5–6 minutes until they are just beginning to brown. Remove them from the oven and wrap in a clean, dry dish towel to keep them soft until you are ready to serve.

For homemade baharat spice blend, put 1 teaspoon each of black peppercorns, coriander seeds, cumin seeds, and whole cloves in a small, dry skillet. Add the seeds from 10 cardamom pods and half a crumbled cinnamon stick and dry-fry the spices until they are lightly toasted. Cool slightly and tip into a spice mill or coffee grinder reserved for grinding spices, and blend until finely ground. Tip into a bowl and stir in 1 teaspoon ground paprika and ½ teaspoon freshly ground nutmeg. Store in an airtight container for up to 1 month.

individual
breads

cinnamon doughnuts

Makes **10 doughnuts**

Time **1½–2½** hours, depending
   on machine, plus shaping,
   rising, and cooking

Dough

1 large **egg**, beaten

1 cup **milk**

2 teaspoons **vanilla extract**

2 tablespoons **unsalted
   butter**, softened

½ teaspoon **salt**

2¾ cups **white bread flour**

¼ cup **superfine sugar**

1¼ teaspoons **instant yeast**

To finish

½ cup **superfine sugar**

1 teaspoon **ground cinnamon**

oil, for deep-frying

Lift the bread pan out of the machine and fit the blade.
Put the dough ingredients in the pan, following the
order specified in the manual.

Fit the pan into the machine and close the lid. Set to
the dough program.

At the end of the program turn the dough out onto a
floured surface and cut it into 10 equal pieces. Shape
each into a ball and space them, well apart, on a large,
greased baking sheet. Cover loosely with oiled plastic
wrap and let rise in a warm place for 30–40 minutes
or until almost doubled in size.

Mix together the sugar and cinnamon on a plate. Put
3 inches oil in a large saucepan and heat it until a
small piece of bread sizzles on the surface and turns
pale golden in about 30 seconds.

Fry the doughnuts, 3–4 at a time, for about 3 minutes,
turning them once until golden on both sides. Drain
with a slotted spoon onto several sheets of paper
towel. Cook the remainder. Roll the doughnuts in the
cinnamon sugar while still warm. Serve freshly baked
with strawberry jelly and whipped cream, if desired.

For doughnuts with chocolate sauce, make the
dough and let rise as above. Place 4 oz chopped
semisweet chocolate in a heatproof bowl with
1 tablespoon butter, 4 tablespoons confectioners' sugar,
and 2 tablespoons milk. Rest the bowl over a pan of
gently simmering water and leave until melted, stirring
frequently until smooth. Fry the doughnuts as above,
draining them and rolling in the spiced sugar. Serve with
little pots of the chocolate sauce.

grissini

Makes **about 32 sticks**
Time **1½—2½ hours**,
    depending on machine,
    plus shaping, rising,
    and baking

Dough

1 cup plus 2 tablespoons
    water
3 tablespoons **olive oil**
1 teaspoon **salt**
3 cups **white bread flour**
1½ teaspoons **superfine
    sugar**
1¼ teaspoons **instant yeast**

To finish

5 teaspoons **sesame seeds**
2 teaspoons **fennel seeds**
1 tablespoon chopped
    rosemary, **basil**, or **chives**
1 **egg yolk**, to glaze
1 teaspoon **sea salt flakes**,
    for sprinkling

Lift the bread pan out of the machine and fit the blade. Put the dough ingredients in the pan, following the order specified in the manual.

Fit the pan into the machine and close the lid. Set to the dough program.

At the end of the program turn the dough out onto a floured surface and cut it into 4 pieces. Leave one piece plain, knead the sesame seeds into the second piece, the fennel seeds into the third, and the chopped herbs into the last piece. Cut each quarter into 8 pieces, then roll each piece into a rope about 10 inches long. Transfer to 2 greased baking sheets. Cover loosely with oiled plastic wrap; leave in a warm place for 30 minutes or until the dough is well risen.

Brush the breadsticks with the egg yolk mixed with 1 tablespoon water. Sprinkle the plain ones with the salt flakes. Bake in a preheated oven, 400°F, for 6—8 minutes or until golden. Transfer to a cooling rack to cool.

For grissini with aromatic salt, crumble half a small bay leaf into a coffee grinder (reserved for grinding herbs and spices) with ½ teaspoon each chopped thyme and rosemary and ¼ teaspoon each celery seeds and dried red pepper flakes. Add 1 teaspoon sea salt flakes and grind lightly. (Alternatively pound using a mortar and pestle.) Stir in another 1 teaspoon sea salt. Make the grissini dough as above, then shape without adding the seeds or herbs. Brush with the egg yolk glaze and sprinkle with the aromatic salt. Finish as above.

fruited teacakes

Makes **8 teacakes**

Time **1½–2½ hours**,
  depending on machine, plus
  shaping, rising, and baking

Dough

1¼ cups **milk**

¼ cup **unsalted butter**,
  softened

½ teaspoon **salt**

1 teaspoon **ground mixed
  spice**

2 teaspoons **vanilla bean
  paste** or **vanilla extract**

2¾ cups **white bread flour**

⅓ cup **light brown sugar**

1¼ teaspoons **instant yeast**

1 cup **mixed dried fruit**, to
  glaze

To finish

beaten **egg**, to glaze
superfine sugar, for sprinkling

Lift the bread pan out of the machine and fit the blade. Put the dough ingredients, except the dried fruit, in the pan, following the order specified in the manual.

Fit the pan into the machine and close the lid. Set to the dough program, adding the dried fruit when the machine beeps.

At the end of the program turn the dough out onto a floured surface and cut it into 8 equal pieces. Shape each piece into a ball and space them, about 1¼ inches apart, on a large, greased baking sheet. Cover loosely with oiled plastic wrap and let rise in a warm place for about 30 minutes or until almost doubled in size.

Brush with beaten egg to glaze and bake in a preheated oven, 425°F, for 15–20 minutes until risen and golden. Transfer to a cooling rack to cool and sprinkle with the superfine sugar. Serve split and buttered.

For iced finger buns, beat 2 eggs and make up to 1¼ cups with milk. Continue to make the dough as above, omitting the mixed spice and dried fruit, and using the milk and egg mixture to replace the 1¼ cups milk. Turn the dough out onto a floured surface and cut it into 8 equal pieces. Shape each into finger roll shapes and arrange them on a greased baking sheet, spacing them about 1½ inches apart. Allow the buns to rise and bake as above. Once cooled, spread the tops with glacé icing, made by mixing together 1 cup confectioners' sugar with 2–3 teaspoons lemon or orange juice.

salted pretzels

Makes **35–40 pretzels**

Time **1½–2½ hours**,
  depending on machine,
  plus shaping, rising,
  and baking

Dough

1 cup plus 2 tablespoons **milk**

1 teaspoon **salt**

2 cups **white bread flour**

⅓ cup **rye flour**

1 tablespoon **superfine sugar**

1 teaspoon **instant yeast**

To finish

4 teaspoons **sea salt**

2 teaspoons **superfine sugar**

Lift the bread pan out of the machine and fit the blade. Put the dough ingredients in the pan, following the order specified in the manual. Fit the pan into the machine and close the lid. Set to the dough program.

Put 2 teaspoons sea salt in a small saucepan with the sugar and 3 tablespoons water. Heat until the salt and sugar dissolve, then turn into a small bowl. Grease 2 baking sheets.

At the end of the program turn the dough out onto a floured surface and roll it out to a rectangle, about 14 x 10 inches. Cover loosely with a clean, dry dish towel and let stand for 20 minutes. Cut the rectangle across at ½ inch intervals. Take a piece of dough and bend the ends around to meet, twisting the ends together. Press the ends down onto the curved side of the rope to shape the pretzel. Use the remaining dough to make more pretzels and place them on 2 large, greased baking sheets. Cover loosely with oiled plastic wrap and leave for an additional 20 minutes.

Bake in a preheated oven, 425°F, for 8 minutes until golden. Brush with the salt glaze and sprinkle with more salt. Cool on a cooling rack.

For garlic & rosemary twigs, make the dough as above, adding 1 crushed garlic clove and 1 tablespoon finely chopped rosemary with the milk. Roll out the dough and cut into 10 inch strips, then through the center into shorter sticks. Brush with 1 egg yolk, mixed with 2 teaspoons water and 1 teaspoon sugar. Place on greased baking sheets, sprinkle with salt, and bake as above.

chorizo & manchego buns

Makes **12 buns**

Time **1½–2½ hours**,
    depending on machine, plus
    shaping, rising, and baking

1 cup **water**

3 tablespoons **olive oil**

4 oz **Manchego cheese**, grated

1 teaspoon **salt**

1 teaspoon ground **hot paprika**

2¾ cups **white bread flour**

2 teaspoons **superfine sugar**

1¼ teaspoons **instant yeast**

4 oz **chorizo sausage**, diced

Lift the bread pan out of the machine and fit the blade. Put the ingredients, except the chorizo, in the pan, following the order specified in the manual.

Fit the pan into the machine and close the lid. Set to the dough program, adding the chorizo when the machine beeps.

At the end of the program turn the dough out onto a floured surface and divide it into 12 equal pieces. Shape each piece into a ball. Cut 12 x 6 inch squares of parchment paper. Push a paper square down into a cup of a muffin pan and drop a ball of dough into it. Repeat with the remainder. Cover loosely with a clean, dry dish towel and leave in a warm place for 30 minutes until risen.

Use kitchen scissors to snip across the top of each bun. Bake in a preheated oven, 425°F, for 20 minutes until risen and golden. Transfer to a cooling rack to cool.

For prosciutto & Parmesan crown, fry 4 oz chopped prosciutto in 1 tablespoon olive oil until lightly browned. Make the dough as above, using ¾ cup grated Parmesan cheese instead of the Manchego and adding the prosciutto when the machine beeps. Once the dough is shaped into balls, fit them into a greased 8 inch round cake pan. Allow to rise and bake as above, but increasing the cooking time to 25–30 minutes. After baking, transfer to a cooling rack to cool and serve, torn into individual buns.

goat cheese & bean mini loaves

Makes **10 loaves**

Time **1½–2½ hours**,
depending on machine, plus
shaping, rising, and baking

Dough

1 cup plus 2 tablespoons
water

3 tablespoons **olive oil**

3 tablespoons snipped **chives**

½ teaspoon **black pepper**,
plus extra for sprinkling

1½ teaspoons **salt**

3 cups **white bread flour**

1 teaspoon **superfine sugar**

1¼ teaspoons **instant yeast**

To finish

⅔ cup frozen **baby fava beans**
or **soybeans**

7 oz soft **goat cheese**, diced

milk, to brush

Lift the bread pan out of the machine and fit the blade.
Put the dough ingredients in the pan, following the
order specified in the manual.

Fit the pan into the machine and close the lid. Set to
the dough program.

Cook the beans in boiling water for 1 minute. Rinse in
cold water and pat dry on paper towels.

At the end of the program turn the dough out onto a
floured surface, sprinkle with the beans and cheese
and knead them into the dough until evenly distributed.
Cut the dough into 10 equal pieces.

Grease 10 individual loaf pans and place them on a
baking sheet. Press each piece of dough into a pan. (If
you don't have any individual pans, shape the dough
into balls and space them slightly apart on the baking
sheet.) Cover loosely with oiled plastic wrap and let rise
in a warm place for 30–40 minutes or until almost
doubled in size.

Brush with a little milk, sprinkle with extra black
pepper, and bake in a preheated oven, 425°F, for
20–25 minutes until risen and pale golden. Transfer
to a cooling rack to cool.

For feta, mint, & cucumber rolls, make the dough as
above, adding 2 tablespoons chopped mint when the
machine beeps. Knead 7 oz crumbled feta cheese and
1 drained and chopped pickled cucumber into the
dough instead of the beans and goat cheese. Shape
into 10 balls and space slightly apart on a greased
baking sheet. Finish as above.

mini dinner rolls

Makes **10 rolls**

Time **1½–2½ hours**,
   depending on machine, plus
   shaping, rising, and baking

Dough

1 cup plus 2 tablespoons
   water
2 tablespoons **unsalted
   butter**, softened
1 teaspoon **salt**
3 cups **white bread flour**
1 teaspoon **superfine sugar**
1¼ teaspoons **instant yeast**

To finish

1 **egg yolk**, to glaze
poppy seeds or **black
   mustard seeds**, **sesame
   seeds**, **fennel seeds**,
   paprika, **rosemary sprigs**,
   coarsely ground Cajun
   spice, and **coarse sea salt**

Lift the bread pan out of the machine and fit the blade. Put the dough ingredients in the pan, following the order specified in the manual. Fit the pan into the machine and close the lid. Set to the dough program. At the end of the program turn the dough out onto a floured surface and cut it into 10 pieces.

Take 2 pieces of dough and shape each into a rope 10 inches long. Roll up each piece to make a spiral. Take 2 pieces of dough and divide each into 3 small balls. Arrange these in a triangle with the balls touching to make clover leaf shapes. Take 2 pieces of dough and shape each into a round. Make 5 or 6 cuts with scissors from the edge to the center of each one. Take 2 pieces of dough and shape each into a rope 9 inches long. Loop 1 end of 1 rope, then thread the other end through the loop to make a knot. Repeat with the other piece. Take 2 pieces of dough and shape into ovals. Make 4 small cuts across the top of each with scissors and insert sprigs of rosemary into them. Arrange the shapes on large, greased baking sheets.

Cover loosely with oiled plastic wrap and leave in a warm place to rise for 20 minutes. Brush with the egg yolk mixed with 1 tablespoon of water and sprinkle with seeds, spices, herbs, or salt. Bake in a preheated oven, 400°F, for 10 minutes until golden. Transfer to a cooling rack to cool.

For pesto & olive dinner rolls, make the dough as above, using 2 tablespoons pesto to replace 2 tablespoons of the water. Add ⅓ cup black or green olives, chopped, when the machine beeps. Shape into individual rolls and bake as above.

spicy swirls

Makes **12 spirals**

Time **1½–2½ hours**,
depending on machine, plus
shaping, rising, and baking

2 teaspoons crushed **flaked dried red peppers**

2 teaspoons **cumin seeds**

1 tablespoon **coriander seeds**

2 teaspoons **fennel seeds**

1 cup plus 2 tablespoons **water**

2 tablespoons **sunflower oil**

1 teaspoon **salt**

3 cups **white bread flour**

1 teaspoon **superfine sugar**

1¼ teaspoons **instant yeast**

1 **egg yolk**, to glaze

Crush the dried peppers, cumin, coriander, and fennel seeds using a mortar and pestle. Reserve 1 teaspoon for sprinkling. Lift the bread pan out of the machine and fit the blade. Put the ingredients in the pan, following the order specified in the manual. Add the crushed spices with the flour.

Fit the pan into the machine and close the lid. Set to the dough program.

At the end of the program turn the dough out onto a floured surface and cut it into 12 equal pieces. Roll each piece into a rope about 12 inches long. Roll each rope into a spiral shape and place on 2 large, greased baking sheets, spacing them well apart. Cover loosely with oiled plastic wrap and let rise in a warm place for 25–30 minutes or until almost doubled in size.

Mix the egg yolk with 1 teaspoon water and brush over the dough. Sprinkle with the reserved crushed spices, following the pattern of the spirals.

Bake in a preheated oven, 425°F, for 8–10 minutes until golden and the bases sound hollow when tapped. Transfer to a cooling rack to cool.

For sesame knots, put 6 tablespoons sesame seeds in a small, dry skillet and heat gently, shaking the pan frequently, until the seeds start to toast. Make the dough as above, using the toasted seeds instead of the crushed spices. Divide the dough into 12 equal pieces and shape each into a rope, about 9 inches long. Tie each into a knot shape and space well apart on the baking sheets. Finish as above, sprinkling the knots with sesame seeds.

mini parsnip loaves

Makes **10 loaves**

Time **1½–2½ hours**,
  depending on machine, plus
  cooking, shaping, rising, and
  baking

2 small **parsnips**, cut into
  chunks
2 tablespoons **olive oil**
large pinch of **saffron
  threads**, crumbled
1½ teaspoons **salt**
2¾ cups **white bread flour**
1 teaspoon **superfine sugar**
1¼ teaspoons **instant yeast**
4 tablespoons chopped
  parsley
1 medium strength **red chili**,
  seeded and thinly sliced
milk, to brush

Cook the parsnips in boiling water for 10 minutes until just tender. Drain, reserving the liquid, and mash the parsnips. Allow to cool.

Measure 1 cup plus 2 tablespoons of the cooking juices, making up the quantity with water if necessary. Lift the bread pan out of the machine and fit the blade. Put the ingredients, except the parsley and chili, in the pan, following the order specified in the manual. Add the mashed parsnips with the liquid. Fit the pan into the machine and close the lid. Set to the dough program, adding the parsley and chili when the machine beeps.

At the end of the program turn the dough out onto a floured surface and cut it into 10 equal pieces. Grease 10 x ⅔ cup dariole molds. Shape each piece of dough into a ball and drop into the prepared molds. Place on a baking sheet and cover loosely with oiled plastic wrap. Leave in a warm place for 25–30 minutes or until the dough has just risen above the tops of the molds.

Brush with milk and bake in a preheated oven, 425°F, for 10–15 minutes until golden and the bases of the bread sound hollow when tapped with the fingertips. Transfer to a cooling rack to cool.

For whole-wheat carrot & onion loaves, cook 2 medium carrots in plenty of water until just tender. Drain and mash, reserving 1 cup plus 2 tablespoons of the cooking liquid. Fry 1 small chopped onion in 1 tablespoon olive oil until tender. Continue to make the bread as above using the carrots and liquid to replace the parsnips and replacing 1¼ cups of the white flour with whole-wheat flour.

cherry tomato & basil buns

Makes **8 buns**

Time **1½–2½ hours**,
depending on machine, plus
shaping, rising, and baking

Dough

1¼ cups **water**

½ cup **basil leaves**

6 tablespoons extra virgin
olive oil

1½ teaspoons **salt**

½ teaspoon **dried oregano**

3 cups **white bread flour**

1 teaspoon **superfine sugar**

1¼ teaspoons **instant yeast**

2 tablespoons **capers**,
rinsed and drained

To finish

4 tablespoons **sundried
tomato paste**

1 lb 2 oz **cherry tomatoes**,
halved

⅔ cup **Greek** or **whole milk
yogurt**

4 tablespoons **mayonnaise**

½ teaspoon **black pepper**

salt

Tear half the basil leaves into small pieces. Lift the bread pan out of the machine and fit the blade. Add the water, 3 tablespoons olive oil, salt, oregano, flour, sugar, and yeast to the pan, following the order specified in the manual.

Fit the pan into the machine and close the lid. Set to the dough program, adding the torn basil leaves and capers when the machine beeps.

At the end of the program turn the dough out onto a floured surface and divide it into 8 equal pieces. Roll each piece roughly into a round shape, about 6 inches across, and space them, about 2 inches apart, on 2 large, greased baking sheets. Cover with oiled plastic wrap and let rise in a warm place for 30 minutes.

Dot with the tomato paste to about ½ inch of the edges. Pile the tomato halves on top. Bake in a preheated oven, 450°F, for about 15 minutes until risen and the tomatoes are soft.

Meanwhile, chop the remaining basil and mix with the yogurt, mayonnaise, pepper, and a little salt. Transfer the buns to serving plates and drizzle with the remaining oil and a little more salt. Serve with the yogurt on the side.

For asparagus & tarragon buns, make the dough as above, adding a handful of tarragon leaves to the dough instead of the basil. Trim 13 oz fine asparagus tips, cutting them in half if long, and blanch in boiling water for 1 minute. Divide the dough as above and roll it out to ovals, each about 7 inches long. After rising, dot with 4 tablespoons pesto and pile the asparagus on top. Drizzle with olive oil and salt to serve.

sour cherry & almond rings

Makes **10 rings**

Time **1½–2½ hours**,
depending on machine, plus
shaping, rising, and baking

Dough

1 large **egg**, beaten

⅔ cup **milk**

⅓ cup **unsalted butter**,
softened

¼ teaspoon **salt**

2 cups **white bread flour**

¾ cup **ground almonds**

¼ cup **superfine sugar**

1¼ teaspoons **instant yeast**

1 cup **dried sour cherries**

To finish

beaten **egg**, to glaze

slivered almonds, for
sprinkling

confectioners' sugar, for
dusting

Lift the bread pan out of the machine and fit the blade.
Put the dough ingredients, except the cherries, in the
pan, following the order specified in the manual.

Fit the pan into the machine and close the lid. Set to
the dough program, adding the cherries when the
machine beeps.

At the end of the program turn the dough out onto a
floured surface and divide it into 10 equal pieces.
Shape each piece into a ball, then press a hole through
the center with your floured finger, gradually enlarging
the hole by rotating your finger.

Space the dough rings about 1½ inches apart on
2 large, greased baking sheets. Cover loosely with
oiled plastic wrap and let rise in a warm place until
almost doubled in size.

Brush the rings lightly with beaten egg and sprinkle
with plenty of slivered almonds. Bake in a preheated
oven, 425°F, for 10–15 minutes or until risen and pale
golden. Transfer to a cooling rack to cool. Serve dusted
with confectioners' sugar.

For pecan & apple rings, make the dough as above,
adding 1 teaspoon mixed spice and replacing the
cherries with ½ cup chopped pecan nuts and ½ cup
chopped dessert apple. After baking mix 1 cup
confectioners' sugar with 2–3 teaspoons water to
make a loose icing and drizzle over the buns.

clementine & fig savarins

Makes **8 savarins**

Time **1½–2½ hours**, depending on machine, plus shaping, rising, and baking

Dough

2 **eggs**, beaten

5 tablespoons **milk**

⅓ cup **unsalted butter**, softened

¼ teaspoon **salt**

1½ cups **white bread flour**

3 tablespoons **superfine sugar**

1 teaspoon **instant yeast**

To finish

1 cup **superfine sugar**

5 tablespoons **Drambuie** or **orange-flavored liqueur**

2 tablespoons **lemon juice**

6 **clementines**, peeled and segmented

4 fresh **figs**, each cut into 6 wedges

Lift the bread pan out of the machine and fit the blade. Put the dough ingredients in the pan, following the order specified in the manual.

Fit the pan into the machine and close the lid. Set to the dough program.

At the end of the program turn the dough out onto a floured surface and divide it into 8 equal pieces. Grease 8 dariole molds or similar size individual metal molds. Press a piece of dough into each mold. Cover loosely with oiled plastic wrap and let rise in a warm place until the dough reaches the tops of the molds.

Bake in a preheated oven, 425°F, for about 15 minutes until risen and golden.

Make the syrup. Put the sugar in a medium saucepan with 2 cups water and heat gently until the sugar has dissolved. Bring to a boil and boil for 5 minutes, then stir in the liqueur and lemon juice. Add the clementines and cook gently for 1 minute. Add the figs and cook for another 30 seconds. Drain the fruits.

Remove the savarins from the molds and spoon 2 tablespoons of the syrup over each. Boil the remaining syrup and reduce it by about half so that is very syrupy. Let cool.

Arrange the savarins and fruits on serving plates and spoon over the syrup to serve.

salt & pepper crusted rolls

Makes **12 rolls**

Time **1½–2½ hours**,
depending on machine, plus
shaping, rising, and baking

1 cup plus 2 tablespoons
water

2 tablespoons **unsalted
butter**, softened

3 cups **white bread flour**

1 teaspoon **superfine sugar**

1¼ teaspoons **instant yeast**

2 teaspoons **sea salt**

2 teaspoons **multicolored
peppercorns**, crushed

1 tablespoon **semolina flour**

milk, to brush

Lift the bread pan out of the machine and fit the
blade. Add the water, butter, flour, sugar, yeast, and
½ teaspoon of the salt to the pan, following the order
specified in the manual.

Fit the pan into the machine and close the lid. Set to
the dough program.

Mix the remaining salt with the pepper and semolina
and sprinkle on a plate.

At the end of the program turn the dough out on
to a floured surface and cut it into 12 equal pieces.
Shape each into a ball and brush the tops lightly with
milk. Dip in the salt and pepper mixture and then space
them about 1½ inches apart on a large, greased baking
sheet. Cover loosely with a clean, dry dish towel and let
rise in a warm place for 30 minutes.

Bake in a preheated oven, 425°F, for about 10 minutes
until risen and golden. Transfer to a cooling rack to cool.

For floury baps, make the dough as above, increasing
the salt in the dough to 1 teaspoon and using milk
instead of water. At the end of the program divide the
dough into 8 equal pieces and shape each into a flat
oval, about ½ inch thick. Place on a floured baking
sheet. Brush lightly with milk and dust with plenty of
flour. Let rise, uncovered, for 30 minutes. Make a deep
impression in the center of each bap and bake as
above until golden around the edges.

devonshire splits

Makes **12 splits**
Time **1½–2½ hours**, depending
   on machine, plus shaping,
   rising, and baking

Dough
1¼ cups **cold water**
2 tablespoons **butter**, at room
   temperature
½ teaspoon **salt**
2 tablespoons **milk powder**
3 cups plus 2 tablespoons
   white bread flour
2 teaspoons **superfine sugar**
1¼ teaspoons **instant yeast**

To finish
beaten **egg**, to glaze
¾ cup **strawberry jelly**
1 cup **clotted cream**
confectioners' sugar, for
   dusting

Lift the bread pan out of the machine and fit the blade. Put the dough ingredients in the pan, following the order specified in the manual.

Fit the pan into the machine and close the lid. Set to the dough program.

At the end of the program turn the dough out onto a floured surface and cut it into 12 pieces. Shape each piece into a ball. Put them on large, greased baking sheets, leaving a little space around each one. Cover loosely with oiled plastic wrap and let rise in a warm place for 20–30 minutes.

Brush the rolls with beaten egg. Bake in a preheated oven, 400°F, for 10 minutes until golden and the bases sound hollow when tapped with the fingertips. Transfer to a cooling rack to cool.

When ready to serve, cut a diagonal slice down through the rolls almost but not quite through to the base. Spoon the jelly into the slit, then add spoonfuls of clotted cream. Transfer to serving plates and dust with confectioners' sugar.

For lemon splits, make and bake the dough as above, adding the finely grated zest of 2 lemons to the dough. To finish, slice the rolls as above and fill with lightly whipped cream and lemon curd.

apple & ginger coils

Makes **12 coils**

Time **1½–2½ hours**,
depending on machine, plus
shaping, rising, and baking

Dough

2 **eggs**, beaten

¾ cup **milk**

2 tablespoons **butter**, at room
temperature

½ teaspoon **salt**

3 cups plus 2 tablespoons
white bread flour

¼ cup **superfine sugar**

1¼ teaspoons **instant yeast**

Filling

13 oz **cooking apples**, peeled
and cored

1 tablespoon **lemon juice**

2 tablespoons **water**

¼ cup **superfine sugar**

¾ cup **luxury mixed dried fruit**

2 tablespoons ready-chopped
candied ginger

To finish

2 tablespoons **superfine
sugar**

4 tablespoons **milk**

confectioners' sugar, for
dusting

Lift the bread pan out of the machine and fit the blade.
Put the dough ingredients in the pan, following the
order specified in the manual. Fit the pan into the
machine and close the lid. Set to the dough program.

Meanwhile, make the filling. Dice the apples and place
in a small saucepan with the lemon juice, water, sugar,
and dried fruit. Cover and simmer for 5 minutes until
they are just beginning to soften. Remove the lid and
cook for 3–5 minutes more until the liquid has
evaporated and the apples are tender and the dried
fruits are plumped up. Stir in the ginger; let cool.

At the end of the program turn the dough out onto
a floured surface. Roll it out to a rectangle,
15 x 12 inches.

Spread the apple mixture over the dough to within
about ¾ inch of the edges. Roll it up, starting from one
of the longer edges.

Cut the dough into 12 thick slices and arrange the
pieces, cut sides up, in 3 rows of 4 coils in a
buttered roasting pan, with a base measurement of
12 x 8 inches. Cover loosely with oiled plastic wrap
and let rise in a warm place for 30 minutes.

Bake in a preheated oven, 400°F, for 20–25 minutes
until golden and the central coils sound hollow when
tapped. When they are almost ready, make the glaze by
heating together the sugar and milk until the sugar has
dissolved. Boil for 1 minute, then brush over the hot
bread. Dust with the confectioners' sugar.

party
breads

ciambella mandorlata

Makes **1 large loaf**
  (about **15** thick slices)
Time **1½–2½ hours**,
  depending on machine, plus
  shaping, rising, and baking

Dough

2 **eggs**, beaten
6 tablespoons **milk**
finely grated zest of 2 **lemons**,
  plus 3 tablespoons juice
⅓ cup **unsalted butter**,
  softened
1 teaspoon **salt**
½ teaspoon **ground cinnamon**
2¾ cups **white bread flour**
⅓ cup **superfine sugar**
1½ teaspoons **instant yeast**

To finish

1 tablespoon **unsalted butter**,
  melted and cooled
1 teaspoon **ground cinnamon**
3 tablespoons **superfine
  sugar**
⅔ cup finely chopped
  blanched almonds
1 **egg yolk**, to glaze

Lift the bread pan out of the machine and fit the blade. Put the dough ingredients in the pan, following the order specified in the manual. Add the lemon zest and juice with the milk.

Fit the pan into the machine and close the lid. Set to the dough program.

Put the melted butter in a bowl and stir in the cinnamon, sugar, and almonds until evenly mixed.

At the end of the program turn the dough out onto a floured surface and cut it in half. Roll each half into a thick rope about 18 inches long. Twist the ropes together and transfer to a large, greased and lined baking sheet, curving the ends round into a crescent shape. Cover loosely with oiled plastic wrap and let rise in a warm place for 50–60 minutes or until risen by at least half again.

Mix the egg yolk with 1 teaspoon water and brush over the dough. Sprinkle with the almond mixture, pressing it gently into the dough. Bake in a preheated oven, 400°F, for about 35 minutes until deep golden, covering with foil if the bread starts to over-brown. Transfer to a cooling rack to cool.

For walnut & orange praline braid, make the dough as above, using orange zest and juice instead of the lemon. For the topping, use chopped walnuts instead of the almonds and light brown sugar instead of the superfine sugar. Finish as above.

greek easter wreath

Makes **1 large loaf** (about
15 chunky slices)
Time **1½–2½ hours**,
depending on machine, plus
shaping, rising, and baking

Dough

2 **eggs**, beaten

¾ cup **milk**

3 tablespoons **brandy**

¼ cup **unsalted butter**, melted

½ teaspoon **salt**

2 teaspoons **caraway seeds**

4 cups **white bread flour**

2 tablespoons **superfine
sugar**

2 teaspoons **instant yeast**

To finish

beaten **egg**, to glaze

1 **egg white**

2 teaspoons **superfine sugar**

5 **hard-cooked eggs**, painted
red with food coloring

⅓ cup whole **blanched
almonds**

Lift the bread pan out of the machine and fit the blade.
Put the dough ingredients in the pan, following the order
specified in the manual. Add the brandy with the milk.

Fit the pan into the machine and close the lid. Set to
the dough program.

At the end of the program turn the dough out on
to a floured surface. Cut it into 3 equal pieces and roll
each piece to a rope, about 20 inches long. Braid the
3 ropes together and carefully transfer to a large,
greased baking sheet, bending the ends round to form
a circular, braided ball of dough. Brush the top lightly
with beaten egg. Cover loosely with oiled plastic wrap
and let rise in a warm place for about 45 minutes or
until almost doubled in size.

Mix the egg white with the sugar and brush all over
the dough. Press the hard-cooked eggs gently into the
top of the dough and decorate with the almonds. Bake
in a preheated oven, 400°F, for about 50 minutes until
the dough sounds hollow when tapped with the
fingertips. Cover with foil during baking if the surface
starts to over-brown. Transfer to a cooling rack to cool.

For honey butter, to accompany the toasted bread
for breakfast, put ½ cup softened unsalted butter in a
bowl and beat until smooth. Add ½ cup honey and
beat well until evenly mixed. Turn into a small dish and
chill until ready to serve.

stollen

Makes **1 small loaf** (about 10
  thick slices)
Time **1½–2½ hours**,
  depending on machine, plus
  shaping, rising, and baking

Dough

¾ cup **milk**
finely grated zest of 1 **lemon**
¼ cup **unsalted butter**,
  softened
¼ teaspoon **salt**
½ teaspoon **ground mixed
  spice**
2¼ cups **white bread flour**
¼ cup **superfine sugar**
1¼ teaspoons **instant yeast**
½ cup **golden raisins**
½ cup **blanched hazelnuts**,
  chopped
⅓ cup **candied peel**, chopped

To finish

8 oz **hazelnut marzipan** (see
  below) or **almond marzipan**
  (see pages 184–5)
confectioners' sugar, for
  dusting

Lift the bread pan out of the machine and fit the blade.
Put the dough ingredients, except the golden raisins,
nuts, and peel, in the pan, following the order specified
in the manual.

Fit the pan into the machine and close the lid. Set
to the dough program, adding the golden raisins,
hazelnuts, and peel when the machine beeps.

Roll the marzipan into a thick log about 10 inches long.

At the end of the program turn the dough out onto
a floured surface and roll it out to an oval, about
12 x 7 inches. Lay the log of marzipan over the
dough slightly to one side of the center. Brush a
long edge with a little water and fold the wider piece
of dough over the filling, pressing it down gently.

Transfer the stollen to a large, greased baking sheet
and cover loosely with oiled plastic wrap. Let rise in a
warm place until almost doubled in size. Bake in a
preheated oven, 400°F, for about 25 minutes until risen
and golden. Transfer to a cooling rack to cool. Dust
generously with confectioners' sugar before serving.

For homemade hazelnut marzipan, grind 1 cup
whole blanched hazelnuts in a food processor. Add
¼ cup superfine sugar and ½ cup confectioners' sugar
to the processor and blend briefly to mix. Add 1 small
egg white and blend until the mixture comes together
to make a paste. Gather into a ball, wrap in plastic
wrap, and keep in a cool place until ready to use.

challah

Makes **1 large loaf**
Time **1½–2½ hours**,
   depending on machine, plus
   shaping, rising, and baking

Dough

¾ cup **water**

2 **eggs**, beaten

¼ cup **unsalted butter**, melted

3 tablespoons **honey**

1 teaspoon **salt**

3 cups plus 2 tablespoons
   white bread flour

1¼ teaspoons **instant yeast**

To finish

1 **egg yolk**, to glaze

2 teaspoons **poppy seeds**,
   for sprinkling

Lift the bread pan out of the machine and fit the blade. Put the dough ingredients in the pan, following the order specified in the manual.

Fit the pan into the machine and close the lid. Set to the dough program.

At the end of the program turn the dough out onto a floured surface. Shape it into a thick rope about 29 inches long. Coil up loosely and put it into an 8 inch greased springform pan. Cover loosely with oiled plastic wrap and leave in a warm place for 45 minutes or until the dough reaches the top of the pan.

Mix the egg yolk with 1 tablespoon of water and brush the surface of the dough. Sprinkle with the poppy seeds and bake in a preheated oven, 400°F, for 30 minutes until the bread is deep brown and sounds hollow when tapped with the fingertips. Check after 10 minutes and cover with foil if over-browning. Transfer to a cooling rack to cool.

For enriched poppy seed & lemon loaf, toast 6 tablespoons poppy seeds in a small, dry skillet until they start to pop. Put in the bread pan with 6 tablespoons water, 5 tablespoons lemon juice, the grated zest of 1 lemon, 2 large eggs, ¼ cup very soft unsalted butter, ½ teaspoon salt, 2¾ cups white bread flour, ¼ cup superfine sugar, and 1¼ teaspoons instant yeast, following the order specified in the manual. Set to a 1½ lb loaf size on a basic white program. Just before baking brush the dough lightly with milk and sprinkle with extra poppy seeds.

panettone

Makes **1 large loaf**

Time **1½–2½ hours**,
depending on machine, plus
shaping, rising, and baking

1 large **egg**, beaten
¾ cup **milk**
finely grated zest of 1 **lemon**
finely grated zest of 1 **orange**
2 teaspoons **vanilla bean
paste** or **vanilla extract**
¼ cup **unsalted butter**,
softened
½ teaspoon **salt**
½ teaspoon **ground nutmeg**
3 cups plus 2 tablespoons
white bread flour
½ cup **superfine sugar**
1½ teaspoons **instant yeast**
1¼ cups luxury **mixed dried
fruit**
confectioners' sugar, for
dusting (optional)

Lift the bread pan out of the machine and fit the blade.
Put the ingredients, except the dried fruit, in the pan,
following the order specified in the manual.

Fit the pan into the machine and close the lid. Set to
the dough program, checking the consistency of the
dough after about 5 minutes kneading. If the dough is
soft and sticky add a little more flour. Add the dried
fruit when the machine beeps.

Grease a 6 inch round cake pan, at least 3½ inches
deep. Line the sides with a triple thickness of
parchment paper, so that it extends 2 inches above
the rim. Grease the paper.

At the end of the program turn the dough out onto a
floured surface and shape it into a ball. Drop the ball
into the pan. Cover loosely with oiled plastic wrap and
let rise in a warm place until the dough reaches the top
of the paper.

Bake in a preheated oven, 400°F, for about 30 minutes
or until risen and golden, covering with foil if the
surface starts to over-brown. Shake the bread out of
the pan and tap the base; it should sound hollow. If
necessary, cook a little longer.

Transfer to a cooling rack to cool. Serve dusted with
confectioners' sugar (if desired).

For pandolce, chop 1 cup candied citron into small
pieces. Roughly chop ⅓ cup blanched almonds. Make
the dough as above, using candied citron and nuts
instead of the mixed dried fruit. Shape the dough and
finish as above.

hot cross buns

Makes **12 buns**

Time 1½–2½ **hours**,
   depending on machine, plus
   shaping, rising, and baking

Dough

1 **egg**, beaten

1 cup plus 2 tablespoons **milk**

3 tablespoons **unsalted butter**, softened

½ teaspoon **salt**

2 teaspoons **ground mixed spice**

3 cups plus 2 tablespoons **white bread flour**

3 tablespoons **light brown sugar**

1½ teaspoons **instant yeast**

⅔ cup **raisins**

To finish

½ cup **all-purpose flour**

4 tablespoons **milk**

2 tablespoons **superfine sugar**

Lift the bread pan out of the machine and fit the blade. Add the dough ingredients, except the raisins, to the pan, following the order specified in the manual.

Fit the pan into the machine and close the lid. Set to the dough program, adding the raisins when the machine beeps.

At the end of the program turn the dough out on to a floured surface and divide it into 12 pieces. Shape each into a ball and space 2 inches apart on a greased baking sheet. Cover loosely with oiled plastic wrap and let rise in a warm place for 30 minutes.

Make the crosses. Beat 4–5 tablespoons water into the flour to make a paste. Put it in a waxed paper pastry bag (or spoon it into the corner of a small polythene bag) and snip off the tip. Pipe crosses over the buns.

Bake in a preheated oven, 425°F, for 15 minutes until risen and golden. Heat the milk and sugar in a pan until the sugar dissolves. Bring to a boil and brush over the buns. Cool on a cooling rack.

For hot cross bun loaf, put 1 cup plus 2 tablespoons milk, 2 tablespoons very soft butter, ½ teaspoon salt, finely grated zest of 1 lemon, 2 teaspoons ground mixed spice, 2¾ cups white bread flour, ¼ cup light brown sugar, and 1½ teaspoons instant yeast in the bread pan, following the order specified in the manual. Set to a 1½ lb loaf size on the sweet program, adding 1⅓ cups luxury mixed dried fruit when the machine beeps. Halfway through baking, pipe a cross on the surface using the mixture above. After baking brush with the glaze.

sweet breads

sweet pineapple & lime loaf

Makes **1 medium loaf**
(about 8 thick slices)
Time **1½–2½ hours**,
depending on machine, plus
shaping, rising, and baking

Dough
¾ cup **water**
2 tablespoons **unsalted
butter**, softened
½ teaspoon **five spice powder**
finely grated zest of 2 **limes**,
plus 4 tablespoons juice
½ teaspoon **salt**
2½ cups **white bread flour**
5 tablespoons **superfine
sugar**
¾ teaspoon **instant yeast**

To finish
10 oz sweetened **semidried
pineapple**, chopped into
small pieces
¾ cup **confectioners' sugar**
pared **lime zest**, for sprinkling

Lift the bread pan out of the machine and fit the blade.
Put the water, butter, five spice powder, lime zest,
3 tablespoons lime juice, salt, flour, sugar, and yeast in
the pan, following the order specified in the manual.
Fit the pan into the machine and close the lid. Set to
the dough program.

At the end of the program turn the dough out onto a
floured surface and divide it into 4 pieces. Grease a
2 lb loaf pan and line the base and long sides with a
strip of waxed paper. Flatten each piece of dough to a
rectangle that is roughly the size of the pan and place
a piece in the base. Sprinkle with one quarter of the
chopped pineapple. Cover with a second layer of
dough. Repeat the layering, finishing with a layer of
fruit. Cover loosely with oiled plastic wrap and let rise
in a warm place until almost doubled in size.

Bake in a preheated oven, 400°F, for 30 minutes or
until risen and golden. Turn out of the pan and return to
the oven for another 5–10 minutes or until the loaf
sounds hollow when tapped with the fingertips. Cover
with foil if the loaf starts to over-brown.

Mix the confectioners' sugar with the remaining lime juice
and drizzle over the bread. Sprinkle with lime zest; let cool.

For pear & ginger loaf with lemon glaze, make the
dough as above, using ground ginger instead of the
five spice powder and lemon zest and juice instead
of lime. Chop 10 oz dried pears. Layer the dough
and pears in the pan. Bake as above. Mix the
confectioners' sugar with 1 tablespoon lemon juice
and drizzle over the bread.

sticky toffee & date loaf

Makes **1 large loaf**

Time **2¾–3½ hours**,
depending on machine, plus
cooking

1½ cups pitted **dates**, roughly
chopped

1 quantity **toffee sauce** (see
below)

1 large **egg**, beaten

¾ cup **milk**

¼ cup **unsalted butter**, softened

¼ teaspoon **salt**

1½ teaspoons **ground mixed
spice**

2½ cups **white bread flour**

1¼ teaspoons **instant yeast**

confectioners' sugar, for
dusting

Put the dates in a small saucepan with 5 tablespoons water. Cover and cook gently for about 5 minutes until the dates have softened and the water has been absorbed. Allow to cool.

Lift the bread pan out of the machine and fit the blade. Put half the toffee sauce in the pan with the remaining ingredients, except the dates, following the order specified in the manual.

Fit the pan into the machine and close the lid. Set to a 1½ lb loaf size on the sweet program (or basic if the machine doesn't have a sweet setting). Add the dates to the pan when the machine beeps.

At the end of the program lift the pan out of the machine and shake the bread out onto a cooling rack to cool. Dust with confectioners' sugar. Serve freshly baked or lightly toasted with the remaining sauce spooned over. If the sauce has become very thick on cooling, it can be heated gently to soften.

For homemade toffee sauce, put ⅔ cup heavy cream in a saucepan with ¾ cup light brown sugar and ⅓ cup unsalted butter. Heat gently, stirring, until the sugar has dissolved and the butter melted. Bring to a boil and let the sauce bubble for 5–8 minutes until the mixture thickens and darkens. Turn into a bowl and allow to cool before using.

blueberry & vanilla braid

Makes **1 large braid** (about
  10 thick slices)
Time **1½–2½ hours**, depending
  on machine, plus shaping,
  rising, and baking

Dough

⅔ cup **water**
2 teaspoons **vanilla bean
  paste**
1 large **egg**, beaten
⅓ cup **unsalted butter**,
  softened
¼ teaspoon **salt**
2¼ cups **white bread flour**
½ cup **ground almonds**
¼ cup **superfine sugar**
1¼ teaspoons **instant yeast**

To finish

½ cup **ricotta cheese**
2 cups **blueberries**
3 tablespoons **superfine
  sugar**
beaten **egg**, to glaze
vanilla sugar, for sprinkling

Lift the bread pan out of the machine and fit the blade. Put the dough ingredients in the pan, following the order specified in the manual. The vanilla bean paste should be added with the liquids and the almonds with the flour. Fit the pan into the machine and close the lid. Set to the dough program.

At the end of the program turn the dough out onto a floured surface and divide it into 3 equal pieces. Roll each piece to a strip about 14 x 5 inches. Spread ricotta over each strip to about ¾ inch of the edges. Sprinkle with 1¾ cups of the blueberries and sprinkle 1 tablespoon sugar over each strip. Bring up the edges over the filling, pinching them together firmly to make 3 thick ropes. Roll them over so the joins are underneath. Braid the strips together, tucking the ends underneath, and carefully lift onto a large, greased baking sheet. Cover loosely with oiled plastic wrap and let rise in a warm place for 40 minutes or until nearly doubled in size.

Brush with beaten egg. Sprinkle with the remaining blueberries and with vanilla sugar. Bake in a preheated oven, 400°F, for 30 minutes or until risen and golden. Cool on a cooling rack.

For red fruit & vanilla loaf, make and shape the dough as above. Use cream cheese instead of the ricotta and 1½ cups mixed dried red fruit (such as cranberries, sour cherries, and strawberries) instead of the blueberries. Before cooking sprinkle with an extra ¼ cup chopped red fruits and with vanilla sugar.

coffee & walnut bread

Makes **1 large loaf**
Time **2¾–3½ hours**,
    depending on machine

2 tablespoons **espresso
    coffee powder**
1 large **egg**, beaten
¼ cup **unsalted butter**, melted
¼ teaspoon **salt**
2¼ cups **white bread flour**
¼ cup **light brown sugar**
1¼ teaspoons **instant yeast**
½ cup **walnut pieces**, lightly
    toasted

Blend the coffee with ⅔ cup boiling water and allow to cool. Lift the bread pan out of the machine and fit the blade. Put the ingredients, except the walnuts, in the pan, following the order specified in the manual.

Fit the pan into the machine and close the lid. Set to a 1½ lb loaf size on the sweet program (or basic if the machine doesn't have a sweet setting). Add the walnuts to the pan when the machine beeps.

At the end of the program lift the pan out of the machine and shake the bread out onto a cooling rack to cool.

For maple butter, to spread over the freshly baked bread, beat together ½ cup soft unsalted butter, 4 tablespoons confectioners' sugar and 1 teaspoon vanilla bean paste or vanilla extract until completely smooth. Beat in 5 tablespoons maple syrup until combined. Turn into a small serving dish and chill until ready to serve.

rich fruit teabread

Makes **1 extra-large loaf**

Time **1½–2½ hours**,
 depending on machine, plus
 shaping, rising, and baking

¾ cup strong **black tea**,
 cooled
1 **egg**, beaten
¼ cup **unsalted butter**,
 softened
½ teaspoon **salt**
finely grated zest of **1 orange**
1 tablespoon **ground mixed
 spice**
2⅓ cups **white bread flour**
⅓ cup **dark brown sugar**
1½ teaspoons **instant yeast**
1¼ cups luxury **mixed dried
 fruit**
⅔ cup ready-to-eat **dried
 apricots**, roughly chopped
⅔ cup chopped **Brazil nuts**
Demerara sugar, for sprinkling

Lift the bread pan out of the machine and fit the blade.
Put the ingredients, except the dried fruit and nuts, in
the pan, following the order specified in the manual.
Add the spice with the flour.

Fit the pan in the machine and close the lid. Set to the
dough program, adding the dried fruits and nuts when
the machine beeps.

At the end of the program turn the dough out onto
a floured surface and shape it into an oval. Grease a
2 lb loaf pan and drop the dough into the pan. Cover
loosely with oiled plastic wrap and let rise in a warm
place for 50–60 minutes or until almost doubled in size.

Sprinkle generously with Demerara sugar and bake in
a preheated oven, 425°F, for 35–40 minutes until risen
and golden. Cover the top with foil if the surface starts
to over-brown. Turn out of the pan and tap the base: it
should sound hollow. If necessary, return to the oven (out
of the pan) for a little longer.

For chunky fruit & nut loaf, put 1 egg, ¾ cup milk,
¼ cup very soft butter, 1 tablespoon molasses,
½ teaspoon salt, 2⅓ cups white bread flour,
1 tablespoon ground mixed spice, ¼ cup dark brown
sugar, and 1¼ teaspoons instant yeast in the bread
pan, following the order specified in the manual. Set
to the sweet program. Add 1 cup luxury mixed dried
fruit and ½ cup roughly chopped almonds when the
machine beeps. At the end of the program shake the
bread out onto a cooling rack to cool.

white chocolate & banana loaf

Makes **1 large loaf**
Time **1–2 hours**, depending
  on machine

8 oz mashed **banana** (about
  2 large bananas)
⅔ cup warm **milk**
¼ cup **unsalted butter**,
  softened
½ teaspoon **salt**
2⅔ cups **white bread flour**
¼ cup **superfine sugar**
2½ teaspoons **instant yeast**
7 oz **white chocolate**,
  chopped
1 cup **pecan nuts**, roughly
  chopped
confectioners' sugar, for
  dusting

Lift the bread pan out of the machine and fit the blade.
Put the ingredients, except the chocolate and nuts, in
the pan, following the order specified in the manual.
Add the mashed banana with the milk.

Fit the pan into the machine and close the lid. Set to
a 1½ lb loaf size on the fast/rapid bake program. Add
the chocolate and pecans when the machine beeps.

At the end of the program lift the pan out of the
machine and shake the bread out onto a cooling rack
to cool. Serve dusted with confectioners' sugar.

For dark chocolate & ginger rolls, put the ingredients
in the bread machine as above, replacing ¼ cup of the
flour with ¼ cup cocoa powder. Reduce the yeast to
1½ teaspoons and add 3 pieces of stem ginger from a
jar, finely chopped. Use chopped semisweet chocolate
instead of the white. Set to the dough program,
adding the chocolate and nuts when the machine
beeps. At the end of the program turn out the dough
and shape into 8 small balls. Space well apart on a
greased baking sheet and cover loosely with oiled
plastic wrap. Leave in a warm place to rise until
almost doubled in size. Bake in a preheated oven,
425°F, for about 15 minutes until risen and lightly
browned. Transfer to a cooling rack to cool and serve
dusted with confectioners' sugar.

sticky chelsea buns

Makes **12 buns**

Time **1½–2½ hours**,
depending on machine, plus
shaping, rising, and baking

Dough

1 **egg**, beaten

1 cup **milk**

¼ cup **unsalted butter**,
softened

½ teaspoon **salt**

finely grated zest of **1 lemon**

3 cups plus 2 tablespoons
white bread flour

⅓ cup **superfine sugar**

1½ teaspoon **instant yeast**

To finish

¼ cup **unsalted butter**,
softened

¼ cup **light brown sugar**

1 teaspoon **ground mixed
spice**

1¼ cups luxury **mixed dried
fruit**

1 inch piece of **fresh ginger
root**, grated

¼ cup **superfine sugar**

Lift the bread pan out of the machine and fit the blade. Put the dough ingredients in the pan, following the order specified in the manual. Fit the pan into the machine and close the lid. Set to the dough program.

Mix together the butter and brown sugar to make a paste. Toss the spice with the fruit and ginger in a bowl.

At the end of the program turn the dough out onto a floured surface and roll it out to a rectangle, about 18 x 10 inches. Spread to the edges with the butter and sugar paste and sprinkle with the fruit mixture. Roll up the dough starting from a long side. Use a sharp knife to cut the log into 12 equal slices.

Grease a shallow 11 x 7 inch baking pan. Arrange the slices in the pan cut sides up, spacing them evenly. Cover loosely with oiled plastic wrap and let rise in a warm place for about 45 minutes or until doubled in size.

Bake in a preheated oven, 400°F, for 25–35 minutes until risen and golden. Cover the buns with foil if they start to over-brown.

Meanwhile, put the superfine sugar in a pan with 6 tablespoons water and heat gently until the sugar dissolves. Bring to a boil and boil for 1 minute. Transfer the buns to a cooling rack and brush them with syrup. Allow to cool.

For chocolate, fruit, & nut buns, substitute lemon zest for orange. Replace the butter paste and fruit mixture with 7 oz chopped chocolate, 1 teaspoon ground ginger, ¾ cup raisins, and ½ cup chopped hazelnuts. Drizzle with melted chocolate.

sour cream & berry bread

Makes **1 large loaf**
Time **2¾–3½ hours**,
   depending on machine

⅔ cup **water**
⅔ cup full-fat **sour cream**
½ teaspoon **salt**
grated zest of 1 **lemon**
2⅔ cups **white bread flour**
3 tablespoons **superfine
   sugar**
1 teaspoon **instant yeast**
⅔ cup mixed **dried cherries,
   blueberries,** and
   cranberries

Lift the bread pan out of the machine and fit the blade.
Put the ingredients, except the mixed fruit, in the pan,
following the order specified in the manual.

Fit the pan into the machine and close the lid. Set to a
1½ lb loaf size on the sweet program (or basic if the
machine does not have a sweet setting). Add the dried
fruits when the machine beeps.

At the end of the program lift the pan from the
machine and shake the bread out onto a cooling rack
to cool.

For berry bread with orange liqueur, put the mixed
dried berries in a bowl and pierce all over with a fork.
Add 3 tablespoons Cointreau or other orange-flavored
liqueur to the bowl. Cover and let steep for about
3 hours until the liqueur has been absorbed. Continue
to make the bread as above, using the grated zest of
1 orange instead of the lemon.

chocolate & pecan spiral

Makes **1 extra-large loaf**

Time **1½–2½ hours**,
depending on machine, plus
shaping, rising, and baking

Dough

2 **eggs**, beaten

¾ cup **milk**

3 tablespoons **unsalted
butter**, softened

½ teaspoon **salt**

3 cups plus 2 tablespoons
white bread flour

¼ cup **superfine sugar**

1½ teaspoons **instant yeast**

To finish

4 oz **semisweet chocolate**,
finely chopped

1 cup **pecan nuts**, roughly
chopped

2 tablespoons **superfine
sugar**

1 **egg yolk**, to glaze

Lift the bread pan out of the machine and fit the blade.
Put the dough ingredients in the pan, following the
order specified in the manual.

Fit the pan into the machine and close the lid. Set to
the dough program.

At the end of the program turn the dough out onto a
floured surface and roll it to an 11 inch square. Sprinkle
with three-quarters of the chocolate and the nuts and
all of the sugar. Roll up the dough, then put it into a
greased 7 cup loaf pan. Cover loosely with oiled plastic
wrap and leave in a warm place for 30 minutes or until
the dough reaches just above the top of the pan.

Mix the egg yolk with 1 tablespoon of water and brush
it over the dough. Sprinkle with the remaining chocolate
and pecan nuts and bake in a preheated oven, 400°F,
for 35–40 minutes until the bread is well risen and
deep brown and sounds hollow when tapped with the
fingertips. Cover with foil after 10 minutes to prevent
the nuts from over-browning.

For brandied prune & chocolate slice, roughly chop
1¼ cups soft pitted prunes and put them in a bowl with
2 tablespoons brandy and steep for 2 hours. Make the
dough as above. Turn the dough out onto a floured
surface and work in the prunes and 4 oz each of dark
and white chocolate. Shape into a log and drop into a
greased 7 cup loaf pan. Cover loosely with oiled plastic
wrap and leave in a warm place until almost doubled in
size. Bake as above. After baking, dust with a mixture of
cocoa powder and confectioners' sugar.

poppy seed, orange, & fig loaf

Makes **1 large loaf**

Time **3–4 hours**, depending on machine

4 tablespoons **poppy seeds**, plus extra for sprinkling

2 **oranges**

1 large **egg**, beaten

¼ cup **unsalted butter**, softened

2⅔ cups **white bread flour**

4 tablespoons **light brown sugar**

1¼ teaspoons **instant yeast**

1¼ cups **dried figs** (stalks removed), halved

⅓ cup chopped **candied orange**

milk, to brush

Lightly toast the poppy seeds in a dry skillet. Grate the zest from the oranges and squeeze the juice. Make the juice up to 1 cup with water.

Lift the bread pan out of the machine and fit the blade. Put the ingredients, except the figs and candied orange, in the pan, following the order specified in the manual.

Fit the pan into the machine and close the lid. Set to a 1½ lb loaf size on the basic white program. Select your preferred crust setting. Add the figs and candied orange when the machine beeps.

Just before baking begins brush the top of the dough lightly with milk and sprinkle with extra poppy seeds. Close the lid gently.

At the end of the program lift the pan out of the machine and shake the bread out onto a cooling rack to cool. Serve freshly baked and buttered.

For seeded banana loaf, cut 2 cups chewy dried banana slices in half. Lightly toast 4 tablespoons sunflower seeds. Make the loaf as above, substituting the sunflower seeds for poppy seeds and the bananas for the figs. Add 2 teaspoons ground mixed spice with the flour.

pine nut, lemon, & cardamom loaf

Makes **1 medium loaf**

Time **1½–2½ hours**,

depending on machine, plus
shaping, rising, and baking

Dough

20 **cardamom pods**

finely grated zest and juice
of 2 **lemons**

1 large **egg**, beaten

¼ cup **unsalted butter**, softened

½ teaspoon **salt**

3 tablespoons **milk powder**

2⅔ cups **white bread flour**

¼ cup **superfine sugar**

1¼ teaspoons **instant yeast**

To finish

1 cup **pine nuts**, toasted

½ cup **slivered almonds**

1 cup **golden raisins**

1 tablespoon **lemon juice**

½ cup **confectioners' sugar**

Grind the cardamom pods using a mortar and pestle to extract the seeds. Discard the shells and grind the seeds to break them up. Put the lemon zest and juice in a measuring cup and make it up to 1 cup with water.

Lift the bread pan out of the machine and fit the blade. Put the dough ingredients in the pan, following the order specified in the manual.

Fit the pan into the machine and close the lid. Set to the dough program.

At the end of the program turn the dough out onto a floured surface and knead in the pine nuts, almonds, and golden raisins until evenly distributed. Shape the dough into a log shape, about 10 inches long, and place it on a large, greased baking sheet. Cover loosely with oiled plastic wrap and let rise in a warm place for about 45 minutes or until almost doubled in size.

Bake in a preheated oven, 425°F, for about 25 minutes until risen and golden and the base sounds hollow when tapped. Cool on a cooling rack.

Beat together the lemon juice and confectioners' sugar to make a thin icing. Drizzle over the bread to decorate.

For orange florentine loaf, make the dough as above, using orange zest and juice instead of the lemon. Mix together 1½ cups slivered almonds, ½ cup natural candied cherries, halved, ⅔ cup raisins, and 1 tablespoon ground ginger. Knead into the dough instead of the pine nuts, almonds, and golden raisins. Once baked, drizzle with melted white chocolate.

pistachio loaf with tropical fruits

Makes **1 large loaf**
Time **2¾–3½ hours**,
   depending on machine

Dough
⅔ cup shelled **pistachio nuts**
¾ cup **mango juice** or
   pineapple juice
1 large **egg**
2 tablespoons **unsalted**
   butter, softened
½ teaspoon **salt**
2⅔ cups **white bread flour**
¼ cup **light brown sugar**
1¼ teaspoons **instant yeast**
5 oz **semidried tropical fruits**,
   such as papaya, mango, and
   pineapple, chopped
¼ cup **candied cherries**

To finish
milk, to brush
confectioners' sugar, for
   dusting

Put the pistachio nuts in a bowl and cover them with boiling water. Leave for 1 minute, then drain and rub between several layers of paper towel to loosen the skins. Peel away the skins and roughly chop the nuts.

Lift the bread pan out of the machine and fit the blade. Put the dough ingredients, except the nuts and fruits, in the pan, following the order specified in the manual.

Fit the pan into the machine and close the lid. Set to a 1½ lb loaf size on the sweet program (or basic if the machine doesn't have a sweet setting). Add the fruits and two-thirds of the pistachio nuts to the pan when the machine beeps.

Just before baking begins brush the top of the dough lightly with milk and sprinkle with the reserved nuts. Close the lid gently.

At the end of the program lift the pan out of the machine and shake the bread out onto a cooling rack to cool. Dust lightly with confectioners' sugar.

For spiced rum butter, to spread over the freshly baked bread, heat ¼ cup confectioners' sugar in a small pan with 1 teaspoon ground cinnamon and 1 tablespoon water until bubbling. Allow to cool slightly. Beat ½ cup soft unsalted butter in a bowl. Add the cinnamon syrup, an additional ½ cup confectioners' sugar, and 2 tablespoons rum. Beat well until smooth and creamy. Turn into a small serving dish and chill until ready to serve.

nectarine & marzipan fruit kuchen

Makes **1 large loaf**

Time **1½–2½ hours**,
   depending on machine, plus
   shaping, rising, and baking

Dough

⅔ cup **water**

1 **egg**, beaten

2 tablespoons **unsalted
   butter**, softened

¼ teaspoon **salt**

1 tablespoon **milk powder**

grated zest of 1 **lemon**

2 scant cups **white bread
   flour**

2 tablespoons **superfine
   sugar**

¾ teaspoon **instant yeast**

To finish

4 oz **marzipan** (see below),
   coarsely grated

1 lb ripe **nectarines**

2 tablespoons **unsalted
   butter**, melted

2 tablespoons **superfine
   sugar**

toasted **slivered almonds**, for
   sprinkling

superfine sugar, for dusting

Lift the bread pan out of the machine and fit the blade. Put the dough ingredients in the pan, following the order specified in the manual.

Fit the pan into the machine and close the lid. Set to the dough program.

At the end of the program turn the dough out onto a floured surface. Press it into a buttered 11 inch fluted removable-bottomed tart pan.

Sprinkle with the grated marzipan. Halve, pit, and thickly slice the nectarines and arrange them over the top. Let rise, uncovered, in a warm place for 40 minutes or until half as big again.

Brush the fruit with melted butter, sprinkle with sugar, and bake in a preheated oven, 400°F, for 15 minutes. Cover with foil, reduce the heat to 350°F, and bake for another 35–40 minutes until the base is cooked through.

Allow to stand in the pan for 10 minutes, then loosen the edges and remove the tart from the pan, keeping it on the base. Transfer to a plate, sprinkle with slivered almonds, and dust with extra sugar. Serve warm.

For homemade marzipan, put ½ cup whole blanched almonds in a food processor and blend until finely ground. Tip into a bowl and stir in 2 tablespoons superfine sugar, ¼ cup confectioners' sugar, ¼ teaspoon almond or vanilla extract, and 2 teaspoons egg white. Mix to a firm paste using your hands.

pear, cinnamon, & raisin kugelhopf

Makes **1 ring loaf** (about
10 slices)
Time **1½–2½ hours**, depending
on machine, plus shaping,
rising, and baking

Dough

⅔ cup **hard cider**
1 large **egg**, beaten
⅓ cup **unsalted butter**, melted
½ teaspoon **salt**
2⅓ cups **white bread flour**
¼ cup **superfine sugar**
1 teaspoon **instant yeast**

To finish

¼ cup **unsalted butter**,
softened
⅓ cup **dark brown sugar**
2 teaspoons **ground cinnamon**
4 ripe **pears**
2 teaspoons **lemon juice**
⅔ cup **raisins**
confectioners' sugar, for
dusting

Lift the bread pan out of the machine and fit the blade. Put the dough ingredients in the pan, following the order specified in the manual. Fit the pan into the machine and close the lid. Set to the dough program.

Mix the butter with the sugar and cinnamon to make a paste. Peel, core, and slice the pears. Toss in the lemon juice to prevent browning.

At the end of the program turn the dough out onto a floured surface and roll it out to a rectangle, about 14 x 10 inches. Spread the spiced butter over the dough almost to the edges and sprinkle with the pears and raisins. Loosely roll up the dough. With the join facing upward bring the ends of the dough to meet and press them together. Thoroughly grease and flour the base and sides of a 6 cup kugelhopf pan or plain ring mold. Drop the dough into the pan.

Cover loosely with oiled plastic wrap and let rise in a warm place for 50–60 minutes or until the dough has risen to the top of the pan.

Bake in a preheated oven, 400°F, for about 35 minutes until risen and deep golden. Leave in the pan for 10 minutes, then loosen the edges with a knife and invert the bread onto a cooling rack to cool. Serve warm or cold, dusted with confectioners' sugar.

For spiced plum kugelhopf, halve, pit, and slice 8 ripe plums. Make the kugelhopf as above, sprinkling the plums over the spiced butter instead of the pears. Roll up and finish as above.

summer fruit cheesecake slice

Makes **8 slices**

Time **1½–2½ hours**,
depending on machine, plus
shaping, rising, and baking

Dough

1 **egg**, beaten

⅔ cup **milk**

1 tablespoon **vanilla bean
paste** or **vanilla extract**

2 tablespoons **unsalted
butter**, softened

1 tablespoon **milk powder**

2 scant cups **white bread
flour**, plus 1 tablespoon

¼ cup **superfine sugar**

¾ teaspoon **instant yeast**

To finish

¾ cup **cream cheese**

¼ cup **superfine sugar**, plus
1 tablespoon for sprinkling

1 teaspoon **vanilla bean
paste** or **vanilla extract**

1 **egg**

1¼ cups **raspberries**

1 cup **strawberries**, hulled
and halved

confectioners' sugar, for
dusting

Lift the bread pan out of the machine and fit the blade.
Put the dough ingredients in the pan, following the order
specified in the manual. Fit the pan into the machine and
close the lid. Set to the dough program.

Beat the cream cheese to soften, then beat in the
sugar, vanilla paste or extract, and egg until smooth.

At the end of the program turn the dough out on
to a floured surface and cut off one quarter. Roll out
the remainder to a round about 11 inches in diameter.
Grease a 9 inch springform cake pan. Press the dough
into the pan so that it comes about 1¼ inches up the
sides, making a shell.

Divide the remaining dough into 10 equal pieces and
arrange them in the shell. Dot the cream cheese
mixture between the dough pieces, then sprinkle with
half the berries. Cover loosely with oiled plastic wrap
and let rise in a warm place until slightly risen.

Bake in a preheated oven, 400°F, for about 45
minutes until the bread is risen and golden. Make sure
the center of the dough is cooked by piercing it with a
knife or skewer. Transfer to a cooling rack to cool.
Serve sprinkled with the remaining fruits and dusted
with confectioners' sugar.

For spiced peach & red currant slice, add
1 teaspoon ground cinnamon instead of the vanilla
paste or extract. Chop 4 ripe peaches into small
chunks and use instead of the berries. After baking,
drizzle the cake with melted red currant jelly and
sprinkle with clusters of red currants.

gooey chocolate nut bread

Makes **8–10 slices**

Time **1½–2½ hours**,
   depending on machine, plus
   shaping, rising, and baking

Dough

1 large **egg**, beaten

⅔ cup **milk**

2 teaspoons **vanilla bean
   paste**

⅓ cup **unsalted butter**,
   softened

¼ teaspoon **salt**

2⅛ cups **white bread flour**

½ cup **ground hazelnuts**

¼ cup **superfine sugar**

1¼ teaspoons **instant yeast**

To finish

¾ cup **chocolate hazelnut
   spread**

¾ cup **hazelnuts**, roughly
   chopped, plus 3
   tablespoons to decorate

beaten **egg**, to glaze

2 oz **semisweet chocolate**,
   chopped

cocoa powder and
   confectioners' sugar, for
   dusting

Lift the bread pan out of the machine and fit the blade.
Put the dough ingredients in the pan, following the
order specified in the manual. Add the ground
hazelnuts with the flour. Fit the pan into the machine
and close the lid. Set to the dough program. Grease an
8 inch removable-bottomed, round cake pan.

At the end of the program turn the dough out onto a
floured surface. Roll one-third of the dough to a
10½ inch round. Place it in the pan so it comes about
1¼ inches up the sides to make a shell.

Dot one-third of the chocolate spread over the base
and sprinkle with one-third of the nuts. Divide the
remaining dough into 3 pieces and roll each to an
8 inch round. Place one layer in the pan and dot with
another third of the chocolate spread and nuts.
Continue layering finishing with a layer of dough.

Brush the dough with beaten egg. Press the chopped
chocolate and reserved nuts into the dough. Cover loosely
with oiled plastic wrap and let rise in a warm place for
45–60 minutes or until about half the size again.

Bake in a preheated oven, 400°F, for 50 minutes.
Cover it with foil if the top starts to over-brown.
Transfer to a cooling rack to cool. Serve dusted with
cocoa powder and confectioners' sugar.

For white chocolate & pecan bread, instead of the
chocolate spread, melt together 7 oz white chocolate,
2 tablespoons unsalted butter, 1 tablespoon corn
syrup, and 2 tablespoons milk. Substitute pecan nuts
for the hazelnuts and white chocolate for the chopped
semisweet chocolate.

lardy cake

Makes **10 thick slices**

Time **1½–2½ hours**, depending on machine, plus shaping, rising, and baking

Dough

1¼ cups **water**

2 tablespoons **lard**, softened

¼ teaspoon **salt**

2 tablespoons **milk powder**

1 teaspoon **ground mixed spice**

2⅔ cups **white bread flour**

2 tablespoons **superfine sugar**

1¼ teaspoons **instant yeast**

To finish

½ cup **lard**, softened

2 tablespoons **unsalted butter**, softened

1½ cups **mixed dried fruit**

⅓ cup chopped **candied peel**

½ cup **superfine sugar**, plus extra for sprinkling

milk, to brush

Lift the bread pan out of the machine and fit the blade. Put the dough ingredients into the pan, following the order specified in the manual.

Fit the pan into the machine and close the lid. Set to the dough program.

At the end of the program turn the dough out onto a floured surface and roll it out to a rectangle, about 16 x 9 inches, with a short end facing you. Using a knife, dot the lard over the dough, then dot over smaller pieces of butter.

Mix together the dried fruit, peel, and sugar and sprinkle over the dough. Press down gently with your hand. Fold the bottom third of the dough over and press down gently, then fold the top third of the dough over to form a rectangle of 3 layers. Turn the dough through 45 degrees and re-roll to a similar-size rectangle. Fold the ends in as before and re-roll to a rectangle slightly smaller than the size of a shallow, greased 11 x 7 inch baking pan. Lift the dough into the pan, cover loosely with oiled plastic wrap, and let rise in a warm place until risen by about half again.

Brush with a little milk and sprinkle with extra sugar. Bake in a preheated oven, 400°F, for about 45 minutes until risen and golden. Leave in the pan for 10 minutes, then transfer to a cooling rack to cool. Serve warm cut into chunky slices.

For lardy cake with ginger, add 3 tablespoons grated fresh ginger root to the pan with the water when making the dough. Chop 3 pieces stem ginger and mix with the dried fruit and sugar. Finish as above.

crumbly blackberry & apple torte

Makes **10 slices**

Time **1½–2½ hours**, depending on machine, plus shaping, rising, and baking

Dough
⅔ cup **apple juice**

1 **egg**, beaten

2 tablespoons **unsalted butter**, softened

1 tablespoon **milk powder**

½ teaspoon **ground mixed spice**

2 scant cups **white bread flour**

¼ cup **superfine sugar**

¾ teaspoon **instant yeast**

To finish
½ cup **all-purpose flour**

3 tablespoons firm **unsalted butter**

5 tablespoons **superfine sugar**

1 lb 2 oz **cooking apples**

1 tablespoon **lemon juice**

1 cup **blackberries**

Lift the bread pan out of the machine and fit the blade. Put the dough ingredients in the pan, following the order specified in the manual. Add the spice with the flour.

Fit the pan into the machine and close the lid. Set to the dough program.

Blend the flour, butter, and 3 tablespoons sugar in a food processor until the mixture starts to bind together with a moist crumbly texture.

At the end of the program turn the dough out onto a floured surface and flatten it out into a circle. Grease a 10½ inch removable-bottomed tart pan. Fit the dough into the pan so the dough comes slightly up the sides.

Peel, core, and slice the apples and toss them with the lemon juice and the remaining 2 tablespoons sugar. Arrange the slices over the dough and sprinkle with the blackberries. Spoon the crumble mixture over the top and bake in a preheated oven, 400°F, for 50–60 minutes until cooked through (test by piercing the cake in the center to check that the dough is cooked). Cover with foil during cooking if the topping starts to over-brown.

For crumbly plum & ginger torte, make the dough as above, adding 2 pieces chopped stem ginger instead of the mixed spice. Break 4 oz gingersnap cookies into a food processor. Add ¼ cup unsalted butter and 4 tablespoons light brown sugar. Blend until the mixture has a coarse, crumble consistency. Once the dough is in the pan, sprinkle with 1 lb pitted and sliced plums. Spoon the gingersnap mixture over the top and bake as above.

date & hazelnut bread

Makes **1 large loaf**

Time **1–2 hours**, depending on machine

1 cup plus 2 tablespoons **warm water**

2 tablespoons **sunflower oil**

1 teaspoon **salt**

2 tablespoons **milk powder**

¼ cup **toasted wheatgerm**

1 cup plus 2 tablespoons **whole-wheat flour**

1¼ cups **white bread flour**

2 tablespoons **dark brown sugar**

2¾ teaspoons **instant yeast**

½ cup **hazelnuts**, toasted and roughly chopped

⅔ cup **pitted dates**, sliced

½ cup **golden raisins**

Lift the bread pan out of the machine and fit the blade. Put the ingredients in the pan, following the order specified in the manual. Add the hazelnuts, dates, and golden raisins with the flour.

Fit the pan into the machine and close the lid. Set to a 1½ lb loaf size on a fast/rapid bake setting.

At the end of the program lift the pan out of the machine and shake the bread out onto a cooling rack to cool.

For fast-baked almond & amaretti bread, roughly chop ¾ cup unblanched almonds. Put 4 oz amaretti cookies in a plastic bag and crush with a rolling pin. Put ¾ cup warm milk, ¾ cup Greek or whole milk yogurt, ¼ cup soft butter, ½ teaspoon salt, 2½ cups white bread flour, 2 tablespoons light brown sugar, and 2½ teaspoons instant yeast in the bread pan. Add the almonds and crushed cookies with the flour. Set to a 1½ lb loaf size on the fast/rapid bake program. After baking, dust with confectioners' sugar.

cherry & frangipane twist

Makes **1 large loaf**

Time **1½–2½ hours**,
depending on machine, plus
shaping, rising, and baking

Dough

1 cup **water**

1 **egg**, beaten

2 tablespoons **butter**, at room
temperature

½ teaspoon **salt**

2 tablespoons **milk powder**

3 cups plus 2 tablespoons
white bread flour

1 tablespoon **superfine sugar**

1¼ teaspoons **instant yeast**

Filling

½ cup **butter**, at room
temperature

½ cup **superfine sugar**

1 **egg**, beaten

1 cup **ground almonds**

½ teaspoon **almond extract**

14 oz can **black cherries**

To finish

3 tablespoons **milk**

3 tablespoons **slivered
almonds**

3 tablespoons **confectioners'
sugar**

Lift the bread pan out of the machine and fit the blade.
Put the dough ingredients in the pan, following the
order specified in the manual. Fit the pan into the
machine and close the lid. Set to the dough program.

Meanwhile, make the frangipane filling by creaming
together the butter and sugar. Add the egg, almonds,
and almond extract and mix together.

At the end of the program turn the dough out onto
a floured surface and roll it out to a rectangle,
15 x 12 inches.

Spread the frangipane over the dough to within about
¾ inches of the edge. Drain the cherries and sprinkle
them over the top, then roll up the dough, starting from
one of the longer edges. Twist the rolled-up dough to
give a corkscrew effect then carefully transfer it to a
greased baking sheet. Cover with oiled plastic wrap
and leave in a warm place for about 30–40 minutes
or until well risen.

Brush with milk, sprinkle with the slivered almonds,
and bake in a preheated oven, 400°F, for about 25
minutes until golden and the bread sounds hollow
when tapped with the fingertips. Cover with foil after
15 minutes if over-browning. Transfer to a cooling rack
and dust with sifted confectioners' sugar. Serve warm
or cold.

For apricot frangipane twist, add the crushed seeds
of 10 cardamom pods to the frangipane paste and
finish as above. Use 12 oz sliced fresh apricots
instead of the cherries.

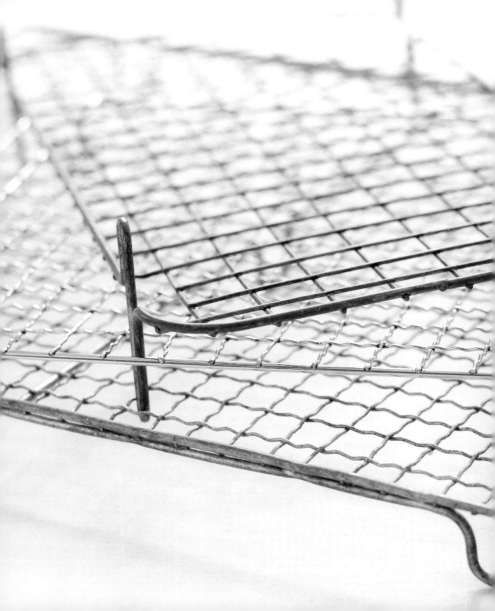

cakes

cherry & almond madeira cake

Makes **8 slices**

Time about **1¼ hours**,
depending on machine, plus
cooking

½ cup **dried black cherries**

5 tablespoons **apple juice**

¾ cup **unsalted butter**,
softened

¾ cup **superfine sugar**, plus
extra for dusting

3 large **eggs**, beaten

2 cups **self-rising flour**

½ teaspoon **baking powder**

1 cup **ground almonds**

1 teaspoon **almond extract**

Put the cherries and apple juice in a small saucepan and heat gently, uncovered, for about 5 minutes until the cherries have plumped up slightly and the juice has been absorbed. Allow to cool.

Lift the bread pan out of the machine and fit the blade. Put the ingredients, except the cherries, in the pan, following the order specified in the manual.

Fit the pan into the machine and close the lid. Set to the cake program. After about 5 minutes use a plastic spatula to scrape the mixture down from the sides and from the corners of the pan. Sprinkle the cherries into the pan once the cake is evenly mixed.

Test the cake after 1¼ hours by inserting a skewer into the center. If it comes out clean the cake is ready. If not, cook a little longer or complete the program.

Transfer the cake to a cooling rack to cool. Serve dusted with extra sugar.

For coffee & walnut madeira cake, omit the cherries, juice, and almond extract. Dissolve 1 tablespoon espresso coffee powder in 2 tablespoons boiling water and add to the pan with the remaining ingredients. Make as above, adding ⅔ cup roughly chopped walnuts to the pan once the cake is evenly mixed. Finish as above.

sticky marmalade cake

Makes **8 slices**

Time about 1¼ **hours**,
   depending on machine

1 cup **hazelnuts**

⅓ cup coarse or fine-shred
   citrus marmalade, plus
   4 tablespoons

5 pieces **stem ginger** from
   a jar, finely chopped

¾ cup **unsalted butter**,
   softened

⅓ cup **light brown sugar**

3 **eggs**, beaten

2 cups **self-rising flour**

1 teaspoon **baking powder**

Grind three-quarters of the hazelnuts in a food
processor. Roughly chop the remainder.

Lift the bread pan out of the machine and fit the blade.
Put the ingredients, except the 4 tablespoons
marmalade, in the pan, following the order specified in
the manual.

Fit the pan into the machine and close the lid. Set to
the cake program. After about 5 minutes use a plastic
spatula to scrape the mixture down from the sides and
from the corners of the pan.

Test the cake after 1¼ hours by inserting a skewer into
the center. If it comes out clean the cake is ready. If
not, cook a little longer or complete the program.

Transfer the cake to a cooling rack. Melt the extra
4 tablespoons marmalade in a small saucepan with
1 tablespoon water. (Sieve the marmalade to remove
the shreds first, if desired.) Brush over the cake and
allow to cool.

For citrus cream cheese cake, make the cake as
above then beat ¾ cup cream cheese in a bowl with
the finely grated zest of 1 orange and 1¾ cups
confectioners' sugar until smooth. Use a spatula to
spread the frosting over the top and sides of the cake.

moist & fruity teacake

Makes **8–10 slices**

Time about **50 minutes**,
   depending on machine,
   plus standing

1⅛ cups luxury **mixed
   dried fruit**

⅔ cup **light brown sugar**, plus
   a little extra for sprinkling

4 tablespoons **malt extract**

2 cups **shredded bran** or
   bran-flake cereal

1½ teaspoons **ground
   mixed spice**

1½ cups **milk**

1¾ cups **self-rising flour**

1 teaspoon **baking powder**

Lift the bread pan out of the machine and fit the blade. Add the dried fruit, sugar, malt extract, cereal, spice, and milk to the pan. Stir gently to mix, then allow to stand for 20 minutes.

Add the flour and baking powder, fit the pan into the machine and close the lid. Set to the cake program. After about 5 minutes use a plastic spatula to scrape the mixture down from the sides and from the corners of the pan.

Test the cake after 50 minutes by inserting a skewer into the center. If it comes out clean the cake is ready. If not, cook a little longer or complete the program.

Transfer the cake to a cooling rack and sprinkle with extra sugar. Allow to cool. Serve sliced and buttered.

For date & pecan teacake, lightly toast 1 cup pecans and roughly chop them along with ¾ cup pitted dates. Put in the bread pan with the sugar, cereal, spice, and milk as above and using date syrup instead of the malt extract. Allow to cool as above before completing.

chocolate fudge slice

Makes **10 slices**

Time about **1 hour**, depending on machine

Cake

¾ cup **cocoa powder**

3 oz **semisweet chocolate**, chopped

⅔ cup **unsalted butter**, softened

1 cup **light brown sugar**

2 large **eggs**, beaten

1¾ cups **self-rising flour**

½ teaspoon **baking powder**

Frosting

7 oz **semisweet chocolate**

1½ cups **confectioners' sugar**

⅔ cup **unsalted butter**, softened

Beat the cocoa powder in a bowl with 1 cup boiling water until smooth. Stir in the chopped chocolate and allow to cool, stirring occasionally, until the chocolate has melted.

Lift the bread pan out of the machine and fit the blade. Put the cake ingredients in the pan.

Fit the pan into the machine and close the lid. Set to the cake program. After about 5 minutes use a plastic spatula to scrape the mixture down from the sides and from the corners of the pan.

Test the cake after 1 hour by inserting a skewer into the center. If it comes out clean the cake is ready. If not, cook a little longer or complete the program. Transfer the cake to a cooling rack to cool.

Make the frosting. Melt the chocolate in a small bowl and allow to cool slightly. Beat together the confectioners' sugar and butter, then beat in the chocolate. Split the cake in half and sandwich with one quarter of the frosting. Transfer to a serving plate and use a spatula to spread the remaining frosting over the top and sides.

For double chocolate fudge slice, make the cake as above, then measure 1 cup heavy cream and pour half into a small saucepan. Heat gently until it bubbles around the edges, then remove from the heat and tip in 1 cup chopped white chocolate. Allow to stand for a few minutes until the chocolate has melted, then stir lightly and turn into a bowl. Leave until cool. Add the remaining cream and beat with a hand-held electric mixer until the mixture just starts to hold its shape. Use to cover the cake.

spicy apple parkin

Makes **8 slices**

Time about **1 hour**, depending
on machine, plus cooking

4 tart **dessert apples**, such as
Granny Smith
5 tablespoons **apple juice**
¼ teaspoon **ground cloves**
½ cup **molasses**
½ cup **corn syrup**
⅓ cup **unsalted butter**,
softened
1 cup **self-rising whole-
wheat flour**
1 cup **self-rising white flour**
1 teaspoon **baking soda**
2 teaspoons **ground ginger**
1 cup **steel-cut oats**

Peel, core, and slice the apples and put the slices in a
small saucepan with the apple juice and ground cloves.
Bring to a boil, reduce the heat, and cook gently,
uncovered, for about 5 minutes or until the apples have
softened slightly. Drain and allow to cool.

Lift the bread pan out of the machine and fit the blade.
Add the molasses, syrup, butter, flour, baking soda,
ginger, and oats to the pan.

Fit the pan into the machine and close the lid. Set to the
cake program. After about 5 minutes use a plastic
spatula to scrape the mixture down from the sides and
from the corners of the pan. Stir in the apples.

Test the cake after 1 hour by inserting a skewer into
the center. If it comes out clean the cake is ready. If
not, cook a little longer or complete the program.
Transfer the cake to a cooling rack to cool.

For brandied prune parkin, roughly chop 1¼ cups
prunes. Make the cake batter as above, omitting the
first step and adding the prunes, 2 tablespoons
brandy, and the grated zest of 1 orange with the rest
of the ingredients.

210

tropical fruit drizzle cake

Makes **8–10 slices**

Time about **1¼ hours**, depending on machine

4 oz **semidried tropical fruits**, such as mango, papaya, and pineapple

4 oz **creamed coconut**

⅔ cup **unsalted butter**, softened

¾ cup **superfine sugar**

3 **eggs**, beaten

finely grated zest of 3 **limes**, plus 4 tablespoons juice

2 cups **self-rising flour**

1 teaspoon **baking powder**

4 tablespoons **superfine sugar,** for sprinkling

Roughly chop the tropical fruit mix if it is in large pieces. If the creamed coconut is in a solid block microwave on medium power for 2–3 minutes to make a soft paste.

Lift the bread pan out of the machine and fit the blade. Add half the chopped fruits, the creamed coconut, butter, ¾ cup superfine sugar, eggs, lime zest, flour, and baking powder to the pan.

Fit the pan into the machine and close the lid. Set to the cake program. After about 5 minutes use a plastic spatula to scrape the mixture down from the sides and from the corners of the pan. Sprinkle in the remaining tropical fruit mixture.

Test the cake after 1¼ hours by inserting a skewer into the center. If it comes out clean the cake is ready. If not, cook a little longer or complete the program. Transfer the cake to a cooling rack to cool.

While the cake is still warm, drizzle over the lime juice and then sprinkle over the sugar. Allow to cool.

For lemon & coconut drizzle cake, omit the tropical fruits and use the zest of 3 lemons instead of the lime. While the cake is cooking blend 4 tablespoons lemon juice with 4 tablespoons superfine sugar. Transfer the cake to a cooling rack and drizzle over the lemon syrup.

cheat's stollen

Makes **1 large loaf**

Time **2¾–3½ hours**, depending on machine

Dough

1 **egg**, beaten

¾ cup **milk**

¼ cup **butter**, melted

½ teaspoon **salt**

grated zest of 1 **lemon**

½ teaspoon **nutmeg**, grated

4 **cardamom pods**, seeds crushed and pods discarded

2⅓ cups **white bread flour**

¼ cup **superfine sugar**

1¼ teaspoons **instant yeast**

½ cup **mixed dried fruit**

¼ cup **candied cherries**, roughly chopped

3 oz yellow **marzipan**, diced

To finish

1 tablespoon **butter**

2 tablespoons **confectioners' sugar**, for dusting

Lift the bread pan out of the machine and fit the blade. Put the dough ingredients, except the dried fruit and marzipan, in the pan, following the order specified in the manual.

Fit the pan into the machine and close the lid. Set to a 1½ lb loaf size on the sweet program.

Add the dried fruit and marzipan when the machine beeps, adding them in small batches so that the blade does not get jammed.

At the end of the program lift the pan out of the machine and shake the bread out onto a cooling rack. Rub the top with the butter and dust heavily with sifted confectioners' sugar. Allow to cool.

For mini stollen bites, make as above but set to the dough program, adding the fruit and marzipan when the machine beeps. Turn out the dough onto a floured surface and roll to fit a greased 11 X 7 inch shallow baking pan. Lift into the pan, pressing the dough into the corners. Cover loosely with oiled plastic wrap and leave until risen by half its size. Bake in a preheated oven, 400°F, for 20–25 minutes until golden. Cool on a cooling rack. Serve cut in squares, generously dusted with confectioners' sugar.

gluten-free
breads

chickpea loaf with crushed spices

Makes **1 large loaf**
Time **1—2 hours**, depending
  on machine

1¼ cups cooked **chickpeas**
1½ cups warm **water**
2 **eggs**, beaten
4 tablespoons **olive oil**
1½ teaspoons **salt**
finely grated zest of 1 **lemon**
1 teaspoon **ground turmeric**
2 teaspoons **coriander seeds**,
  crushed
2 teaspoons **cumin seeds**,
  crushed
¾ cup **cilantro leaves**,
  chopped
2½ cups **wheat- and gluten-
free bread flour**
2 teaspoons **superfine sugar**
2 teaspoons **instant yeast**

Crush the chickpeas, either in a food processor or by mashing them in a bowl with a fork.

Lift the bread pan out of the machine and fit the blade. Put the ingredients in the pan, following the order specified for gluten-free breads in the manual. The chickpeas should be added with the liquids.

Fit the pan into the machine and close the lid. Set to a 1½ lb loaf size on the fast/rapid bake program.

At the end of the program lift the pan out of the machine and shake the bread out onto a cooling rack to cool.

For chili & herb butter, to spread on the bread, beat ½ cup softened butter in a bowl. Add 1 seeded and finely chopped mild chili, 3 tablespoons snipped chives, 2 tablespoons finely chopped parsley, 1 tablespoon chopped mint, and a little salt. Beat well until evenly mixed, then turn into a small dish. Cover and chill until ready to serve.

simple gluten-free white bread

Makes **1 large loaf**

Time **1–2 hours**, depending
  on machine

Dough

2 **eggs**, beaten

1½ cups warm **milk**

1 teaspoon **lemon juice**

2 tablespoons **unsalted
  butter**, softened

1½ teaspoons **salt**

2½ cups **gluten-free white
  bread flour**

¾ cup **rice flour** or **quinoa
  flour**

1 tablespoon **superfine sugar**

2 teaspoons **instant yeast**

To finish

melted **butter**, to brush

sesame seeds or **poppy
  seeds**, for sprinkling

Lift the bread pan out of the machine and fit the blade.
Put the dough ingredients in the pan, following the
order specified for gluten-free breads in the manual.

Fit the pan into the machine and close the lid. Set
to a 1½ lb loaf size on the fast/rapid bake program.

At the end of the program lift the pan out of the
machine and shake the bread out onto a cooling rack.
Brush the top with butter and sprinkle with sesame or
poppy seeds.

For seeded gluten-free white bread, lightly toast
3 tablespoons sesame seeds in a dry skillet until
lightly toasted. Add to the bread pan with the flour
and 2 tablespoons each of flax seeds, sunflower
seeds, and pumpkin seeds. After removing the
bread from the pan, brush with butter and sprinkle
with extra seeds.

roasted red pepper cornbread

Makes **1 large loaf**

Time **1–2 hours**, depending
 on machine, plus cooking

1 **red bell pepper**, cored,
 seeded, and quartered
1 tablespoon **olive oil**
2 **eggs**, beaten
1½ cups **milk**, warmed
¼ cup **unsalted butter**, melted
1 teaspoon **salt**
½ cup grated **Parmesan
 cheese**
1 large, mild **red chili**, seeded
 and finely chopped
1 teaspoon **white wine
 vinegar** or **malt vinegar**
¾ cup fine **ground corn** (masa
 harina)
2 scant cups **wheat- and
 gluten-free bread flour** with
 added natural gum
2 teaspoons **superfine sugar**
2 teaspoons **instant yeast**
4 **scallions**, chopped
melted **butter**, to brush

Put the pepper quarters, skin side up, on the broiler
rack, brush with oil, and broil for 10 minutes until the
skins are blackened. Wrap in foil, allow to cool, then
peel off the skins and roughly chop the flesh.

Lift the bread pan out of the machine and fit the blade.
Put the ingredients in the pan, following the order
specified for gluten-free breads in the manual. Add
the chopped peppers and scallions with the sugar
and yeast.

Fit the pan into the machine and close the lid. Set to a
1½ lb loaf size on a fast/rapid bake program.

At the end of the program lift the pan out of the
machine and shake the bread out onto a cooling rack.
Brush the top with the butter and brown under the
broiler, if desired. Allow to cool.

glazed pear & cinnamon loaf

Makes **1 large loaf**

Time **1–2 hours**, depending on machine, plus soaking

⅔ cup **dried pears**, chopped

⅔ cup **golden raisins**

1⅔ cups strong, hot **tea**

1 **egg**, beaten

2 tablespoons **unsalted butter**, softened

¼ teaspoon **salt**

2 teaspoons **ground cinnamon**

2⅓ cups **gluten-free white bread flour**

⅓ cup **light brown sugar**

1½ teaspoons **instant yeast**

confectioners' sugar, for dusting

Put the chopped pears and golden raisins in a bowl with the hot tea and allow to soak for 1 hour.

Lift the bread pan out of the machine and fit the blade. Put the ingredients in the pan, following the order specified for gluten-free breads in the manual. Add the golden raisins with the pears and liquid.

Fit the pan into the machine and close the lid. Set to a 1½ lb loaf size on the fast/rapid bake program.

At the end of the program lift the pan out of the machine and shake the bread out onto a cooling rack. Serve freshly baked or toasted and buttered.

For white chocolate & ginger loaf, omit the pears and increase the golden raisins to 1¼ cups, soaking them in 1⅔ cups strong hot tea. Chop 5 oz white chocolate into pieces. Continue as above, substituting ¼ cup of the gluten-free flour with cocoa powder and adding the chopped chocolate when the machine beeps.

sunflower & apricot bread

Makes **1 large loaf**

Time **1–2 hours**, depending on machine

1 cup warm **water**

2 **eggs**, beaten

4 tablespoons **sunflower oil**

⅔ cup **Greek** or **whole milk yogurt**, plus extra to serve (optional)

1 teaspoon **salt**

3 cups **wheat- and gluten-free bread flour** with added natural gum

2 tablespoons **light brown sugar**

2 teaspoons **instant yeast**

⅓ cup **sunflower seeds**

¾ cup ready-to-eat **dried apricots**, diced

confectioners' sugar, for dusting

Lift the bread pan out of the machine and fit the blade. Put the ingredients in the pan, following the order specified for gluten-free breads in the manual. Add the seeds and apricots with the sugar and yeast.

Fit the pan into the machine and close the lid. Set to a 1½ lb loaf size on fast/rapid bake program.

At the end of the program lift the pan out of the machine and shake the bread out onto a cooling rack. Dust with confectioners' sugar, then broil until browned. Allow to cool. Serve with more Greek yogurt, blueberries and honey (if desired).

For breakfast loaf with tropical fruits, chop 6 oz semidried tropical fruits (such as mango, papaya, and pineapple) into small pieces. Make the bread as above, using the chopped fruits instead of the apricots and sunflower seeds and using ⅔ cup tropical fruit-flavored yogurt instead of the plain yogurt.

sundried tomato & herb bread

Makes **1 large loaf**
Time **1–2 hours**, depending
  on machine, plus soaking

½ cup **buckwheat**
1 cup warm **water**
2 **eggs**, beaten
⅓ cup **sundried tomato paste**
2 tablespoons **unsalted
  butter**, softened
1 teaspoon **celery salt**
2 scant cups **gluten-free
  bread flour**
2 teaspoons **superfine sugar**
2 teaspoons **instant yeast**
small handful of chopped
  fresh herbs, such as
  parsley, chervil, rosemary,
  chives, and oregano
1 cup **sundried tomatoes** in
  olive oil, drained and sliced

Put the buckwheat in a bowl and add ½ cup boiling water. Allow to soak for 20 minutes until the water has been absorbed.

Lift the bread pan out of the machine and fit the blade. Put the buckwheat in the pan with all the ingredients, except the herbs and sliced sundried tomatoes, following the order specified for gluten-free breads in the manual.

Fit the pan into the machine and close the lid. Set to a 1½ lb loaf size on a fast/rapid bake program. Add the herbs and sliced sundried tomatoes when the machine beeps.

At the end of the program lift the pan out of the machine and shake the bread out onto a cooling rack to cool.

For pesto & pine nut bread, toast ½ cup pine nuts in a dry skillet and allow to cool. Finely chop 1 tablespoon rosemary. Soak the buckwheat in the water as above and put it in the machine with 2 eggs, 1 cup warm water, 5 tablespoons green pesto, 2 tablespoons very soft butter, 1 teaspoon celery salt, 1 teaspoon freshly ground black pepper, the pine nuts, rosemary, 2 scant cups gluten-free bread flour, 2 teaspoons superfine sugar, and 2 teaspoons instant yeast. Continue as above.

roasted vegetable loaf with wild rice

Makes **1 small loaf**

Time **1¾–2 hours**, depending on machine, plus cooking

5 oz **mixed roasted vegetables**, drained if packed in a jar with oil, or homemade (see below)

¼ cup **wild rice**

3 tablespoons **olive oil**

2 **eggs**, beaten

1 cup **milk**

1¼ cups **cornmeal**

1 cup **rice flour**

1 teaspoon **salt**

1 tablespoon **wheat-free baking powder**

1 teaspoon hot **paprika**, plus extra for sprinkling

Roughly chop the vegetables if they are in large pieces. Cook the rice in boiling water for about 20 minutes until just tender. Drain and allow to cool.

Lift the bread pan out of the machine and fit the blade. Put the ingredients, except the roasted vegetables, in the pan, following the order specified in the manual.

Fit the pan into the machine and close the lid. Set to the cake program. After about 5 minutes use a plastic spatula to scrape the mixture down from the sides and from the corners of the pan. Sprinkle in the vegetables and a little extra paprika once the loaf is evenly mixed.

Test the loaf after 1¾ hours by inserting a skewer into the center. If it comes out clean the loaf is ready. If not, cook a little longer or complete the program.

At the end of the program lift the pan out of the machine and shake the loaf out onto a cooling rack to cool. Serve warm, buttered, if desired.

For homemade roasted vegetables, seed 3 mixed bell peppers and cut them into chunks. Arrange in a roasting pan with 2 thinly sliced zucchini and 1 small red onion cut into wedges. Drizzle with 2 tablespoons olive oil and sprinkle with 1 teaspoon chopped thyme and 1 teaspoon crushed fennel or coriander seeds. Roast in a preheated oven, 400°F, for 50–60 minutes until tender and beginning to brown. Allow to cool then refrigerate for up to 3 days.

herb bread

Makes **1 large loaf**
Time about **1–2 hours**,
   depending on machine,
   plus cooking

5 oz **parsnips**
1⅔ cups warm **water**
2 tablespoons **olive oil**
1 teaspoon **salt**
1¼ cups **chickpea flour**
2 scant cups **gluten-free bread flour**
4 tablespoons chopped **mixed herbs**
1 teaspoon **superfine sugar**
2½ teaspoons **instant yeast**

Peel and dice the parsnips. Cook them in a saucepan of boiling water for 10 minutes, then drain and mash.

Lift the bread pan out of the machine and fit the blade. Put the ingredients in the pan, following the order specified for gluten-free breads in the manual. Add the mashed parsnip with the water.

Fit the pan into the machine and close the lid. Set to a 1½ lb loaf size on the fast/rapid bake program.

At the end of the program lift the pan out of the machine and shake the bread out onto a cooling rack to cool. If the bread looks pale when you take it out of the machine, brush the top with a little melted butter or oil and broil for a few minutes until browned.

For spiced potato loaf, use the same quantity of mashed potato to replace the parsnip. Crush 2 teaspoons each of cumin and coriander seeds using a mortar and pestle and mix with ½ teaspoon dried red pepper flakes. Add to the pan instead of the mixed herbs and replace the salt with celery salt. Continue as above.

chili corn bread

Makes **1 large loaf**
Time about **1¾–2 hours**,
  depending on machine

2 **eggs**, beaten
⅔ cup **plain yogurt**
1¼ cups **milk**
¼ cup **unsalted butter**,
  softened
½ cup grated **Parmesan
  cheese**
1 tablespoon **superfine sugar**
1 scant cup **yellow cornmeal**
2 cups **all-purpose flour**
3 teaspoons **baking powder**
1 teaspoon **baking soda**
1 teaspoon **salt**
black pepper
2 large whole **dried chilies**,
  finely chopped
6 **scallions**, finely chopped

Lift the bread pan out of the machine and fit the blade. Put the ingredients, except the chilies and scallions, in the pan, following the order specified for gluten-free breads in the manual.

Fit the pan into the machine and close the lid. Set to the cake program. After about 5 minutes use a plastic spatula to scrape the mixture down from the sides and from the corners of the pan. Add the chilies and scallions.

Test the bread 15 minutes before the end of the program by inserting a skewer into the center. If it comes out cleanly, the bread is ready. If not, leave until the program ends and then retest.

Lift the pan out of the machine and shake the bread out onto a cooling rack to cool. Serve with bowls of chili, if desired.

For five spice corn bread, omit the chilies from the recipe above and use a finely chopped red onion instead of the scallions. Crush together using a mortar and pestle, 1 teaspoon dried red pepper flakes, 2 teaspoons cumin seeds, 2 teaspoons coriander seeds, 1 teaspoon black mustard seeds, and 1 teaspoon celery seeds. Tip into a dry skillet and heat for a couple of minutes to lightly toast the seeds. Add to the bread pan with the flour.

index

acknowledgments

Executive Editor: Nicola Hill
Senior Editor: Lisa John
Executive Art Editor: Penny Stock
Designer: Cobalt
Photographer: William Shaw
Home Economist: Joanna Farrow
Props Stylist: Liz Hippisley
Production Controller: Carolin Stransky

Special photography: © Octopus Publishing Group Limited/William Shaw.
Other photography: © Octopus Publishing Group Limited/Ian Wallace 25, 47, 65, 87, 89, 141, 143, 175, 223, 227; /Stephen Conroy 23, 29, 45, 96, 101, 105, 117, 127, 153, 177, 185, 235.